THE AMATEUR ASTRONOMER'S CATALOG
OF 500 DEEP-SKY OBJECTS

Volume One

THE AMATEUR ASTRONOMER'S CATALOG OF 500 DEEP-SKY OBJECTS

Volume One

Ronald J. Morales

AZTEX Corporation   P O Box 50046   Tucson, AZ 85703-1046

This book is dedicated to Mom and Dad

Photo Credits

Cover:
Meade Instruments (Star Photo)

Inside Photos:

Martin C Germano
David Healy
Michael J Coulton
Ben Mayer
James McGaha
Jack Newton
Pierre Schwaar

ISBN 0-89404-076-6

Library of Congress Catalog Card No. 83-73052

Copyright © 1986 by Ronald J. Morales
Copyright © 1986 by **AZTEX** Corporation

All rights reserved. No part of this book may be reproduced or transmitted in any form or by any means, electronic or mechanical, including photocopying, recording or by any information storage or retrieval system, without permission in writing from the publisher.

Printed in the United States of America

AZTEX Corporation
P O Box 50046, Tucson, AZ 85703-1046

FOREWORD

Deep-sky astronomy began when some lonely Chaldean shepherd first glimpsed a pale, misty streak among the stars of Andromeda—and wondered. Such objects, which came to be called 'nebulae' or 'little clouds' by ancient astronomers, were rarities among the seemingly countless congregation of the stars, and even a century after the first telescopes came into use, the number of true 'deep-sky' objects discovered was less than twenty. The now famous catalogue of Charles Messier, published in 1781 boosted this number over the hundred mark, and any modern amateur observer will have tried his 'prentice hand' at finding them all for himself.

The next step along this high celestial road was in fact a giant's leap by that titan among astronomers, William Hershel, who in the years 1786—1802 discovered no less than 2500 *new* nebulae and star clusters. That the amateur of today can follow profitably in Herschel's footsteps is primarily due to the remarkable advances in modern telescope design and manufacture. In fact, the possessor of an eight to ten-inch reflector could hope to observe most of the Herschel objects and more beside.

This task, however, is a challenge of a different order to that of 'Messier-hunting': It requires patience, dedication and skill, especially if one is to avoid the perils and frustrations of mis-identification. It is here that a competent guide becomes an asset which not only avoids much time-wasting effort but also provides further incentive when it is most needed.

The author of this book is well qualified to supply much guidance; Ron Morales is a deep-sky observer of wide experience and ability; he has contributed to several well-known astronomical journals, and in particular provided numerous observations and telescope drawings to the *Webb Society Deep-sky Observer's Handbook*. His practical expertise in observing technique will prove valuable to all who wish to explore this exciting field of observation, and the extensive catalogue he provides will enable observers to compare their own new-found results with those of a dedicated and perceptive observer. Here is a richly-rewarding enterprise for all who wish to take up the challenge of exploration in the deeper territory of the night sky: I wish you all clear skies—and good hunting.

Kenneth Glyn Jones, FRAS
President, Webb Society

CONTENTS

Introduction 9
Observing Technique 11
Observing Tips 15
Astronomy and Communities: 17
    The Impact of Lighting Practices
Observing Forms 19
    Bright Diffuse Nebula 20
    Dark Nebula 21
    Galaxy 22
    Globular Cluster 23
    Open Star Cluster 24
    Planetary Nebula 25
A Beginners Guide to Planetary Nebulae 27
Selected Objects 30
    Galaxies, Planetary Nebulae, Bright Nebulae, Open Clusters,
    Globular Clusters, and Dark Nebulae
Table #1: Estimated Minimum Telescope Aperture 32
Table #2: Planetary Nebulae Classification 33
Table #3: Planetary Nebulae for the Small Telescope 34
Table #4: Telescopes Used in the Catalog Section 35
Table #5: Messier Objects in the Catalog 36
Table #6: Objects Listed in the Catalog 37
New General Catalog (NGC) 47

Telescopic Observations of Non—NGC Objects........ 107
   Index Catalog (IC)...107
   Dark Nebulae..111
   Miscellaneous Observations...................................112
   Miscellaneous Notes...113
   Virgo Cluster..114
   Fornax Galaxy Group..118

Keys To Tables and Catalog Section................... 120

Glossary... 121

Deep Sky Observers Check List...................... 122

Recommended Reading................................ 123

Telescopes & Accessories............................. 124

Deep Sky Objects Found.............................. 125

Failed To See List..................................... 127

INTRODUCTION

Astronomy is one of the most fascinating studies that man can encounter. As with most sciences, there are many branches, each related to and covered under the one word "Astronomy."

Then too, there is a distinction to be made between the *professional* astronomer and the *amateur* astronomer. Though the size and type of equipment and the resources that today's professional has at his or her disposal far outweigh those of the amateur, the amateur and professional still share a common bond—the desire for the knowledge, understanding and excitement that Astronomy has to offer us.

For myself, the art of finding and observing deep-sky objects has brought an unparalleled joy into my life. Keeping my observations in a permanent written form has only added to that joy.

Often amateurs new to deep-sky observing will look at a few of the brighter well-known objects and stop there. Many amateurs, however, will attempt to observe all of the objects on the famous Messier List—110 objects at last count. From there, the serious deep-sky observer will turn to the bible of deep-sky observers........the *New General Catalog of Nebulae and Clusters of Stars*.

Commonly referred to as the NGC, this is a listing of all deep-sky objects known up to the year 1887. Containing 7840 objects, these observations come from many of the famous early observers including William and John Herschel. Two sections added on at a later date are included as part of the *New General Catalog*. The first section is called the Index Catalog (IC$_1$) and includes 1529 objects found from the years 1888 to 1894. The objects listed in the Index Catalog do not follow the numerical sequence of the NGC, but instead start with number one (1). The next add-on section is called the Second Index Catalog, known as the IC$_2$. Containing 3857 objects found from the years 1895 to 1907, the Second Index Catalog does follow the numerical sequence of the IC$_1$—the first entry in the IC$_2$ beginning with the number 1530. It is important to mention that many of the 3857 objects listed in the IC$_2$ were found photographically. Because of this, many of the objects listed will not be seen visually, although some of the objects listed can be seen visually through amateur sized telescopes. The total number of objects in the combined Index Catalogues is 5386, while the combined NGC/IC listings give a total of 13,226 deep-sky objects! There are some objects that are actually listed twice (under two separate numbers) and there are some non-existent objects. But on the whole, this catalog is accurate and extremely useful. The *New General Catalog* is a virtual treasure house full of information on deep-sky objects for the serious amateur astronomer.

I've taken a look at many of the objects listed in the *New General Catalog* and come away with my own observations. This book contains 500 deep-sky objects having NGC numbers. Additionally, some IC objects and others are listed. In the catalog section of this book you will find my own interpretation of these objects as seen through amateur sized telescopes. This section will best be utilized at the telescope. It may help in identifying a deep-sky object when two or more are in the telescope's field. The general description alone may be sufficient to identify a lone object in the field of view. A list of selected objects, taken from the catalog section, may help the amateur decide on which objects to view first. A section on observing techniques is given for those amateurs new to the realm of deep-sky observing—I hope you find it useful. I have included a section on the often times ellusive planetary nebulae, for those amateurs who would like to observe these objects. Hopefully, the veteran deep-sky observer will find the catalog section both useful and interesting. This catalog section is composed of visual observations made in the early 1970s, as seen through amateur sized instruments. These observations were made in and about southern Arizona and occasionally in old Mexico. All observations were made at the eyepiece of the telescope and are not retouched. The coordinates given for the deep-sky objects are for 1950 except where noted. As many veteran deep-sky observers are using one or more star atlases with this epoch, these coordinates should prove useful.

When an amateur first starts observing deep-sky objects, he or she is usually faced with many unanswered questions. What objects should I observe? What objects can I see through my telescope? How do I find this object in my field? What can I expect to see in my scope? The purpose of this book is to assist new deep-sky observers who may have similar questions.

The 500 NGC objects listed in the catalog section were the first such objects that I had observed and recorded, many of them are not at all difficult with the small to medium sized telescope. Many amateurs may find this list helpful, especially after they have found all of the Messier Objects which are included in this catalog.

I hope to help make deep-sky observing an enjoyable aspect of amateur astronomy. If this book helps other amateurs, then it was well worth the time and effort........Good Luck!

Ronald J. Morales
March, 1986

OBSERVING TECHNIQUE

Besides his telescope, the serious amateur needs a few more "tools" before he can successfully scan the heavens.

One item he cannot be without is a good star atlas along with its star catalog. A good star atlas should include the stars down to *at least* 6th or 7th magnitude. The fainter the stars shown, the more useful the atlas. Along with the stars, our atlas should include many deep-sky objects including galaxies, planetary nebulae, clusters, globulars, and bright and dark nebulae. Constellation boundaries are also useful to the amateur. An important point to consider when buying an atlas is its convenience for use at the telescope. An atlas that is inconvenient to use will not be used. I have always found individual star charts much more convenient to use at the telescope than star maps which are bound in a book. The individual star chart can be removed from its package and placed on a flat surface near the telescope. Here it can be referred to often. If necessary, two or more charts can be put together, side by side, and used as one larger chart. The individual charts can also be removed from the table and used at the eyepiece or even held up against the sky and compared to the stars visually. The star catalog is useful in that it contains data on all of the objects shown in the star atlas.

Another useful tool the amateur can use is a list of deep-sky objects as seen by other amateurs. This list of objects will help the amateur in identifying a particular deep-sky object, especially if he is seeking it for the first time. It is also useful when he is planning out his night's observing to see which objects would be visible through a particular aperture scope and which objects are easy to see. He may just take pleasure in reading or comparing another's observation of that particular object. It will certainly tell him what to expect with his telescope. The catalog section of this book gives you *my* personal observations of over 500 deep-sky objects. They were made with telescopes ranging from a pair of binoculars to a 16-inch. However, most of the observations were made with telescopes in the 8-inch to 10-inch range. These observations were made in either southern Arizona or Mexico. Whenever possible, the object was observed near my local meridian. The nights were usually very dark and clear.

Now that the amateur has these important tools, there are a few others he will find useful. A folding card table for holding the star charts near the telescope can also hold your oculars, flashlight, pen and pencil, coffee....etc. A flashlight with a red covering over the lens is very helpful. The red light does not hurt your night vision as does white light. Of course, keep the red flashlight beam dim, so that you do not have a bright beam of red light. I always take a pair of binoculars with me when I go observing. Over the years, I have found that the binoculars really help when searching for faint guide stars while star hopping around the heavens, not to mention the beautiful views they afford of the night sky. If you don't have a pair of binoculars, you can use the finderscope on your telescope. Lastly, you'll find a clock is invaluable when recording your observations.

Once the amateur has all of the tools he needs for successful observing.....then what?

The next thing we need to do is to find a good observing site...an important step that many amateurs fail to consider. A good observing site is free from extraneous light or man-made, heat-rising objects. Try to avoid the light from areas with high sky glow, building lights, lighted signs, headlights from auto or airplane traffic, or heat from buildings, cars, construction equipment...etc. Look for areas that are dark and free from distractions: national parks, monuments, forests or wilderness areas.

A dark site is important because the extraneous light from a less than ideal site will hurt your "seeing" ability through the telescope. Extraneous light such as sky-glow as seen near a city will be seen in your telescope when viewing objects near this light pollution. This light will cause the background sky in your field of view to lighten, having two very noticeable adverse effects. First, it can wash out detail in a bright object that might otherwise have been seen. Second, it can brighten up the background sky considerably—enough to completely conceal a faint object.

Another annoyance to the observer is wind. When the wind comes up you can either wait it out or if it's annoying enough...pack up and go home. Having the telescope sway from side to side while we are trying to make an important observation is futile.

Now that we see just how important a good observing site is...we can be patient in finding one. Traveling 50 miles or more is really not too extravagant—especially not for that "ideal" site. Of course, it is advisable to have more than one observing site. The ones less desirable are usually the ones we find closer to home.....maybe even the backyard? But the really good site is used when you have some serious observing to do. A good observing site is something to be cherished! By using a dark site you are getting the most out of your scope. The ideal situation would be to observe from a dark site under a moonless, clear and dark sky! After all of my years of visual observing, I fully believe that observing from a dark site under clear dark skies is as important as the telescope aperture used!

After having gone through the trouble of finding a good observing site, you certainly will want to take full advantage of it. Try to observe when the sky looks especially clear, usually after a cold front has passed. After heavy rains, the air is left clean and relatively dust free. Observing when there is no moon visible is another plus.

When looking at the night sky, look for an indication of clarity, such as the Milky Way. Does the Milky Way look bright and vivid? What is the faintest visual star you can see overhead using only your naked eye? Are the bright stars twinkling more than usual? This could be an indication of unsteady air which may inhibit observing very faint objects.

After filling all the requirements for a good night's observing, try to spend all night observing with the telescope. I have found that the hours from around midnight to four a.m. are the best. These are the hours that I do my best observing because the seeing seems to be improved.

Now that we have all of our observing conditions in a near ideal state, we should begin to plan out our night's observing. Using a good star atlas, pick out one section of the sky to observe. I usually try to limit myself to one constellation each time I go observing, choosing a different one each time. When picking out a section of the sky, try to choose an area that will be overhead for the hours you plan to observe. An object placed on your zenith or anywhere along your local meridian should have less distortion than an object nearer your horizon. When you choose the objects you plan to observe try to include some new objects that you have not seen before. My own observing list usually contains about ten objects that I have not yet seen, along with the objects I wish to re-observe. This way, you are always seeing new and different objects. Having your objects listed on a sheet, along with any pertinent data you might wish, is very helpful. It helps to guide you while observing so that you are constantly observing and not standing around with your hands in your pockets! Some other data you may wish to have on your list are magnitude of object, size, constellation, type of object.... Once you become used to using an observing sheet such as this, you will feel lost without one.

Now we're ready to start observing. The bright objects on our list will not be difficult to find. But what about the fainter, more elusive objects? In order to locate these we need to prepare ourselves and our telescopes. Make certain that your main telescope and your telescope finder are *exactly* in line. I usually choose a terrestrial object to sight my scope in because it doesn't move. A telephone pole, large rock or other immovable object will work. Use a high power in the main scope when adjusting the two scopes. Now you know that whatever object you place on your finderscope crosshairs will also be in your high power field. Switch your main scope to a low power wide field ocular. Return to your observing list and choose a faint object. From here go to your star chart and locate the object. Be sure to use your flashlight with its red filter so not to ruin your night vision. When you have located the object on your star chart, try to find some bright stars near the object. If possible locate two bright stars, one on either side of the object. If there are no bright stars then look for a fainter star in the 4th to 6th magnitude range. Here again, try to place the faint object between two stars. Once you find two stars that are visible to the naked eye on either side of the object...stop. Now try to identify these two stars in the night sky. Your binoculars or finderscope will help when searching for the correct stars.

Let's call these two stars that you've found in the sky, star A and star B. Now, go back to your star chart and draw an imaginary line from star A to star B. See where the faint object lies in respect to this line. Is the object bisected by this line? Is the object off to one side of your line...etc. After discovering just where the object lies in relation to your imaginary line, transpose this to the night sky. Looking at stars A and B, draw an imaginary line between them in the sky. Find the "spot" where the faint object lies in respect to your line. Now set the crosshairs of your finderscope at this "spot." The faint object will now lie somewhere close to or in your low power field of view. It may be necessary to switch to a medium power to actually see the faint deep-sky object, but at least you have the correct field of view. Some times a little "sweeping" with a low power ocular will be required to find an object. But any object, no matter how faint, can be found by using this method, known as the sky comparison method.

Sometimes there are no visible stars in the vicinity of your chosen object...what then? If you use your binoculars and a good star chart, you can always find some faint stars that form a visible pattern or group, easily distinguishable on your chart and in your binoculars. Star hopping, which is a continuation of the sky comparison method, is another way to locate faint objects. Go from one bright star to stars (usually fainter) closer to the object in question, until you identify a star near the object.

Once you have found the object and observed it, are you finished? Well, not really. Why not record that observation? Remember, an observation worth making is worth recording. Pen and paper are usually used but a small tape recorder is also handy. Observations can be made at the eyepiece with a recorder...to be written down at your leisure.

Whatever method you choose, be sure to include certain data with your observations. Items you want to include are: the name of the object, type of object, telescope used, focal length, oculars used, date of your observation. At the beginning of an observing session I record the observing site, seeing conditions, faintest naked eye star visible overhead along with its magnitude. The magnitude of this star is ascertained from the star catalog. I also include the time that I make each and every observation, but this a personal preference item. When you are actually making the observation, try to include the following: Brightness of the object, size, shape, color, ease of seeing it in the field and other objects in your field (galaxies, clusters, etc). Include anything that you, the observer, feel is important. After all, this is *your* observation. When I make my observations, where applicable, I include other aperture scopes in which the object was also seen. This is especially useful when recording smaller aperture scopes compared to the main scope.

As you start to observe more and more, you will gradually notice an improvement in your observations. You will actually begin to see more detail as you become more experienced in the art of visual observing. One place that this change will become apparent is in your written observations. After a period of time, say two years, compare your most recent observations with those you made in the beginning. You *will* see a difference. You *are* improving! Not only will you see more through your telescope but you will know what to look for. The observing methods described here are guidelines only and should be individually adjusted to suit one's particular needs. These methods are an important first step in making an enjoyable hobby just that much more satisfying.

I have included a list of 46 deep-sky objects which I found particularly interesting or impressive. This group was selected from the catalog section and is divided in the following manner; Galaxies- 9, Planetaries- 14, Bright Nebulae- 11, Open Clusters- 7 and Globular Clusters- 5. You will at once notice the large number of planetary nebulae. This is because these objects are indeed interesting to observe. The amateur needs to give more attention to these often passed-over objects. A separate section deals with planetary nebulae for the beginner.

OBSERVING TIPS

1) *Dark Observing Site*: Choose a site that is as free as possible from manmade lights, and wind. A low horizon in the direction away from any artificial lights (like a city), is a plus. Choose areas such as: Parks, wilderness areas, national monuments, campgrounds, farmlands, etc. Areas of low population flow may also be considered.

2) *Optics*: Make certain that the optics in your telescope are aligned and clean. A basic point but one that is *very* important.

3) *Finderscope*: Be sure that your finderscope is *exactly* aligned with your main telescope. Find an easy bright object and center it in your main telescope. Be sure to use a high power ocular, in the 8mm to 10mm area, when doing this procedure. Once the easy object is centered in the main scope, adjust the finderscope so that the object is centered on the crosshairs. This is indeed a very important step, especially when star hopping from one object to the next.

4) *Oculars*: Use good quality, good formulae oculars. Besides the alignment of your optics the seeing capability of your scope is also dependent upon the quality of your optics, including your oculars and the seeing conditions. Keep your oculars clean and if possible keep them in a dust proof case or box when at your observing site. A small wooden box can be made or even a fishing box of plastic or metal construction can be used. If possible, try to have a wide assortment of different ocular focal lengths. The most powerful ocular usable on a particular object will vary from night to night, dependent on the seeing conditions. Throughout years of visual deep-sky observing, I have found that for each different type of telescope, aperture and focal length, there is one ocular that is perfect for general viewing. I have found this to be a 16mm ocular for the telescopes that I use. I also use this ocular for sweeping an area while searching for a particular object.

5) *Star Charts*: A good set of star charts which are convenient to use at the telescope is a must. I have found the *Skalnate Pleso Atlas* to be exceptionally well suited. The new *Sky Atlas* (Tirion), which replaces the *Skalnate Pleso*, is also an excellent choice. It is important that the star

charts lie flat so they can be placed on a flat surface and referred to as necessary, without having to search for a particular chart time and time again.

6) *Flashlight*: A flashlight with a red lens is necessary for viewing your star chart while not hurting your night vision. A piece of red color transparent candy wrapping works well over a flashlight lens.

7) *Moonless Night*: Observe deep-sky objects when there is no moon. The scattered sky glow from the moon will lighten your field of view and this brighter background sky may wash out a particular object. If the object is faint it may be missed where otherwise it might have been seen.

8) *Failed To See List*: Keep an accurate list of deep-sky objects that you were unable to find. On a particularly clear night, try searching for the objects on this list. . . . you may be surprised to find some. Besides the object's name include telescope aperture, focal length and the ocular used.

9) *Record of Observations*: An accurate record of all of your visual observations makes a nice addition to any amateur's library and is interesting to read over at a later date. By reading over your observations at a later date you can actually follow the improvement of your observing skills. Your observations will be more accurate and organized. This will become one of our most treasured books.

10) *Local Meridian*: Whenever possible try to observe deep-sky objects when they are on your local meridian. This is especially important for objects that pass overhead. When looking directly overhead, at the zenith, you are looking through less atmosphere, than when you are looking at or near the horizon. Less atmosphere means less pollutants, unsteadiness of the air and less diffraction.

11) *Cold Fronts*: It has been my experience that after a cold front or severe rain the sky becomes beautifully transparent and calm. Some of the best observing nights I've had have been after such weather conditions.

12) *Early Hours*: My written observations have shown me that, for my area, predawn hours seem to be the best for clarity and steadiness of the air. The hours between two a.m. to four a.m. are particularly well suited to deep-sky observing. Of course, these hours may not be as good for observing elsewhere; they are purely subjective observations on my own part.

13) *Card Table*: A folding card table is an excellent item to have. This table is easy to carry and can be placed close to the telescope. On this table you can put your star atlas, opened to the correct chart, your eyepiece box, flashlight, pencil and paper, recorder, etc.

14) *Binoculars*: One very important accessory that has proven itself over and over again is a good pair of binoculars. When searching for a faint visual guide star or star group, binoculars are indispensible. Almost any size binocular can be used but I have found the following to be better than most: 7 x 50, 10 x 50, 7 x 35.

15) *Diffraction Grating*: A diffraction grating is especially useful in identifying planetary nebulae that would otherwise be stellar or nearly so. The

diffraction grating is placed between the observer's eye and the ocular. It is then rotated until the stars show a small but obvious spectrum. Tilting the grating parallel to the ground may also help. The stars will show small spectrums while a planetary will show a duplicate image of itself...no spectrum. Instead of a diffraction grating, some amateurs use a small prism in essentially the same manner.

16) *Averted Vision*: Use averted vision when searching for a faint object or while trying to see detail on an object. By averted vision we mean the art of not looking directly at the object but rather look off to one side. Most people can actually see fainter objects using this method.

ASTRONOMY AND COMMUNITIES:
THE IMPACT OF LIGHTING PRACTICES

Modern astronomical research requires siting telescopes on very high mountaintops, in areas where there is a maximum number of cloudless days. The Southwest is the only area in the mainland United States, and one of only *four* areas in the world, that satisfies these requirements.

The dark skies on which these observatories rely have continually deteriorated over the past 50 years, to the point that all of the major observatories in the Southwest are seriously threatened by the sky glow from neighboring communities.

The brightening of the night skies at these observatories has paralleled the growth of the surrounding communities; The Mt. Wilson sky is now comparable to that illuminated by the full moon. The Lick Observatory sky is now as bright as the Mt. Wilson Observatory sky was 25 years ago. The Palomar Observatory sky is now as bright as the Lick sky was 15 years ago.

(Indeed, the very bright sky over Mt. Wilson was one of the prime factors in the decision by the Carnegie Institute of Washington to cease operations at Mt. Wilson June, 1985.)

The sky glow contributed by a community to a nearby observatory depends principally on two factors: the population of the community and the distance of the community from the Observatory. The amount of light coming from a community is closely tied to its population. If one doubles the population, the amount of sky glow doubles, and for a given-sized community, the closer it is to an observatory, the larger its contribution will be to the sky glow.

The amount of sky glow experienced by the major observatories in the Southwest results from the lights produced by a combination of nearby communitites and large, more distant communities. For example, over 30% of the sky glow at Lick Observatory is contributed by communities other than the city of San Jose. The city of San Diego is the single biggest contributor of sky glow to the Palomar Observatory, but much closer, smaller communities also contribute significantly to the sky glow. The city of Tucson is the biggest contributor to the sky glow of Kitt Peak, but significant sky glow can be seen coming from the Phoenix Metropolitan Area, three times more distant but with five times more population. Thus, the problem of increasing sky glow at observatories concerns many communities in the Southwest, not just the handful of big cities to which this issue has been first addressed.

The efficiency of ground-based telescopes is now determined solely by the aperture of the telescope and the level of sky background illumination. Unless effective action is taken to control the quantity and kind of light emitted from neighboring communities, modern astronomical observations will no longer be possible in the mainland United States.

To assess the current outdoor lighting practices in the Southwest, a survey was distributed to 130 cities in six Southwestern states: Arizona, California, Colorado, Nevada, Utah and New Mexico (no respondents). One hundred and three cities (79% of the sample) participated in the study, responding to the following three questions: a) What is the current usage of Mercury Vapor (MV) lamps?; b) What is the current usuage of High Pressure Sodium (HPS) lamps?; and c) What percentage of the lighting system in a city is owned by a utility?

Upon examining the data on a state by state basis, a significant trend emerges: Most of the cities in California have already converted their lighting systems to HPS; only 15% of 64 cities in California and MV lamps comprising *more* than 40% of their lighting systems. In contrast, only a small percentage of the 35 cities in Arizona, Colorado, Nevada and Utah have MV lamps comprising *less* than 40% of their current lighting systems. It is apparent from other data collected on this survey that the relatively early conversion to HPS lamps in California was due to action by the utilities—not government ordinance.

Information from the survey indicate that most of the cities anticipate no need for lighting ordinances. The major exceptions to this are cities, both large and small, that are located near the major observatories in California and Arizona. A total of 23 cities in all have considered light control measures, and nine of these have light control ordinances.

In order to preserve our ability to see the night sky—we—the amateur astronomers, need to make ourselves heard. It is apparent most municipalities will not automatically institute lighting ordinances, therefore we need to initiate these ordinances, on a local level. The information on this page was excerpted from the report *Astronomy and Communities: The Impact of Lighting Practices*. A copy may be obtained by writing to: Arizona State University, Tempe AZ 85287.

OBSERVING FORMS

The observing forms shown on the following pages are intended to give the amateur a basic example of what to look for when observing a particular type of deep-sky object. It is important that the amateur making the observation note the name of the object, the telescope used along with its focal length and oculars used, and the seeing conditions of the sky. A common scale in use is ratings from 1 to 10, with 10 being the best seeing. Of course, the amateur may choose to devise his or her own scale for seeing.

Next, we have some questions that would relate to that observation. As you will see, some questions can be asked for all of the deep-sky objects. The last question shown, the one related to other objects in the field, is optional. I have included it because I have found it rather useful to know what other objects may be within a field of view.

The section labeled *description* is the heart of the observation. This is where the amateur can ask questions, make any comments or any comparisons that he or she desires. Try to include all possible information especially items that appear unusual, impressive or interesting.

Near the bottom of the form, you will find a circle. This is to be used at the telescope for a drawing of the field of view. A drawing is optional but extremely useful. Normally only one drawing is necessary, usually made with the ocular which gives the best overall view.

For the Planetary Nebula you will notice two circles, one low power and one high power. Because most planetaries are so small, we use a high power field to see some of the fine detail often present. A low power field is used in helping the amateur *locate* this planetary nebula among the stars. Since planetaries are often very small, many will appear starlike and indistinguishable among the field stars. Here in our low power field, a small arrow will immediately show where the planetary is located—a useful chart when searching for this same planetary at a later date.

These Observing Forms should be used as a *guide only*. The serious observer may wish to add more questions such as the Right Ascension, Declination, Magnitude, Constellation, etc.

NOTE:
Your field orientation may differ depending upon type of telescope used.

BRIGHT DIFFUSE NEBULA

OBSERVATION SHEET

NGC/IC NO.:

DATE: TIME: SEEING(1-10):

TELESCOPE: OCULAR(S):

Questions to be answered in "Description."
1) How difficult is this object to see?
2) What is the overall shape?
3) Does any one or more sections of this nebula appear brighter or darker than the rest?
4) Is any part of the outer edge of this nebula sharply defined?
5) Any obvious stars involved in this nebula?
6) What power in the telescope gives the best overall view of this object?
7) Any suggestions for observing this object?
8) Are there any other deep-sky objects in the field? If so, what are their names?

DESCRIPTION:

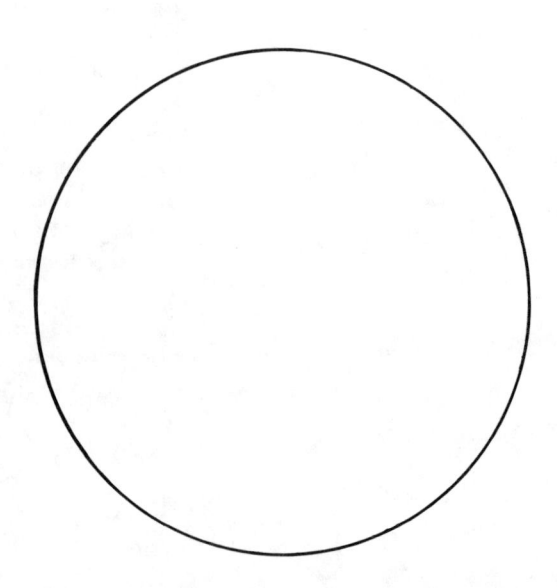

FIELD DRAWING AND NOTES
OCULAR:

DARK NEBULA
OBSERVATION SHEET

NGC/IC NO.:

DATE:　　　　　　TIME:　　　　　　SEEING(1-10):

TELESCOPE:　　　　　　　　　　　OCULAR(S):

Questions to be answered in "Description."
1) How difficult is this object to distinguish from the background?
2) What is its overall shape, size?
3) Are any distinguishing features seen (stars or bright nebulosity involved with this object)?
4) What power in the telescope gives the best overall view of this object?
5) Any suggestions for observing this object?
6) Are there any other deep-sky objects in the field? If so, what are their names?

DESCRIPTION:

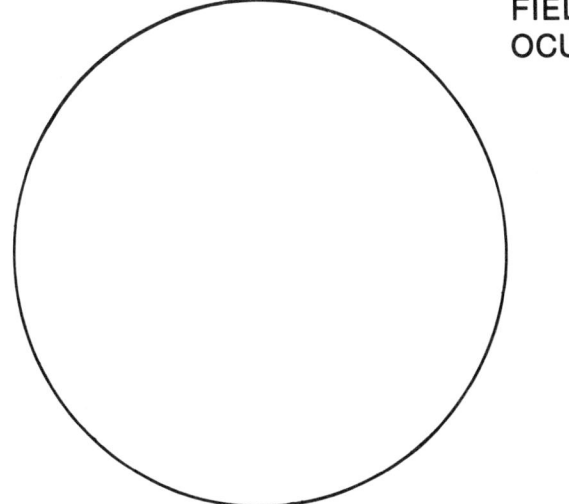

FIELD DRAWING AND NOTES
OCULAR:

GALAXY

OBSERVATION SHEET

NGC/IC NO.:

DATE:　　　　　　TIME:　　　　　　SEEING(1-10):

TELESCOPE:　　　　　　　　　　OCULAR(S):

Questions to be answered in "Description."
1) Can this galaxy be seen with direct vision, or is averted vision required?
2) What is the overall shape of this galaxy?
3) Is a core noticeable? Is it compact or stellar?
4) Are the edges of the outer envelope sharp or diffuse?
5) Can any detail or mottling be seen in the outer envelope (bright or dark patches, foreground stars)?
6) Are there any other deep-sky objects in the field? If so, what are their names?

DESCRIPTION:

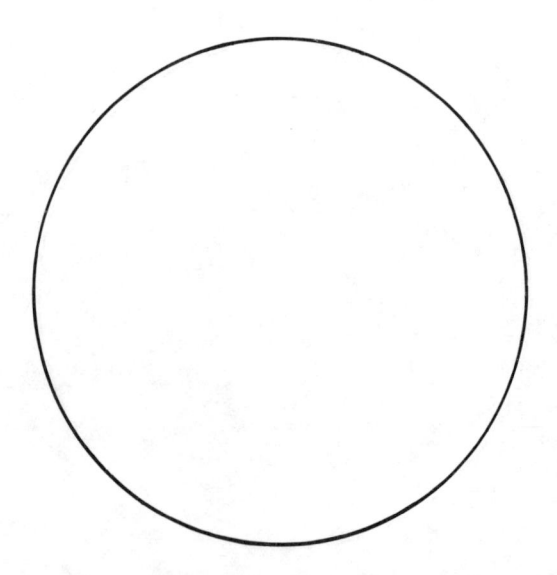

FIELD DRAWING AND NOTES
OCULAR:

GLOBULAR CLUSTER
OBSERVATION SHEET

NGC/IC NO.:

DATE: TIME: SEEING(1-10):

TELESCOPE: OCULAR(S):

Questions to be answered in "Description."
1) Can this object be seen easily?
2) What is its overall shape, size?
3) Is this globular cluster highly or loosely concentrated?
4) Is any part of this globular cluster resolved into stars, or is some mottling seen?
5) Is the core area unusually bright, compact or not distinguishable?
6) Are there any other deep-sky objects in the field? If so, what are their names?

DESCRIPTION:

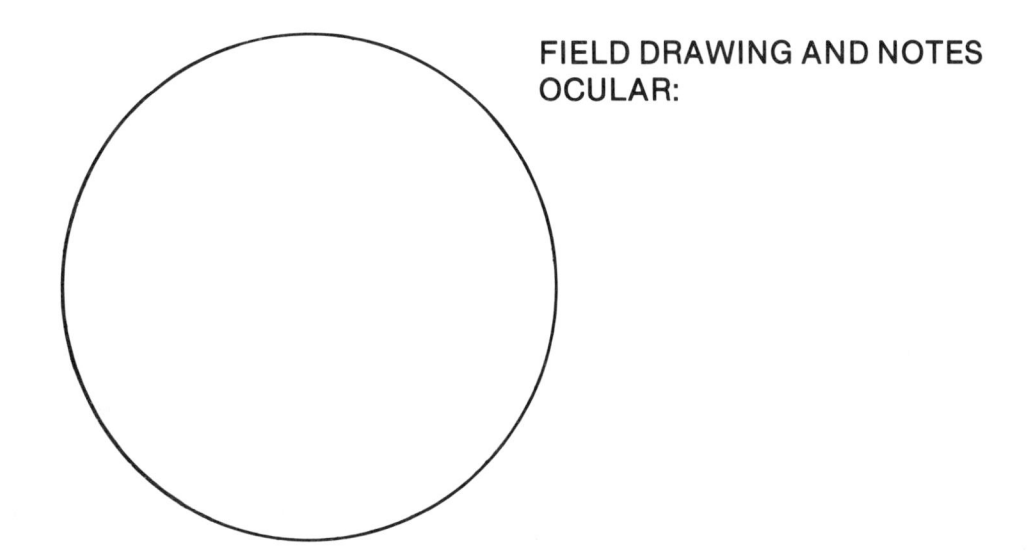

FIELD DRAWING AND NOTES
OCULAR:

OPEN STAR CLUSTER

OBSERVATION SHEET

NGC/IC NO.:

DATE: TIME: SEEING(1-10):

TELESCOPE: OCULAR(S):

Questions to be answered in "Description."
1) Can this cluster be seen easily distinguished from the background stars?
2) Does the entire cluster fit into your field of view? What power are we using?
3) What is the overall shape of this cluster?
4) Are there stars more concentrated in any one particular area?
5) Is there any particular area where you notice a absence of stars in this cluster?
6) Is this cluster resolved fully or is there some background nebulosity noticed?
7) Are there any particularly bright stars involved in this cluster? If so, do they show any color (red, orange, etc.).
8) Are there any other deep-sky objects in the field? If so, what are their names?

DESCRIPTION:

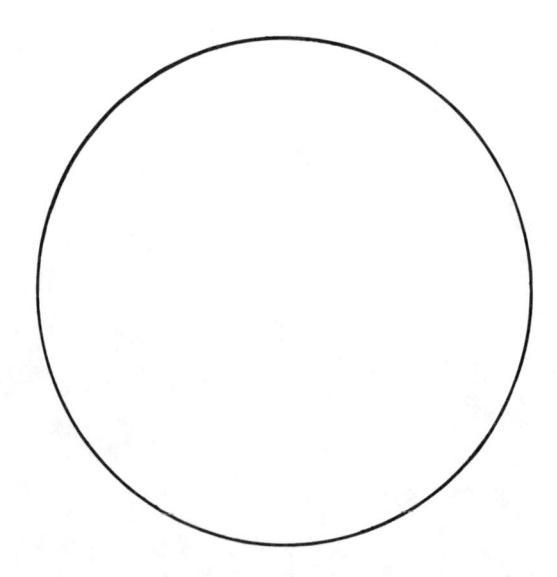

FIELD DRAWING AND NOTES
OCULAR:

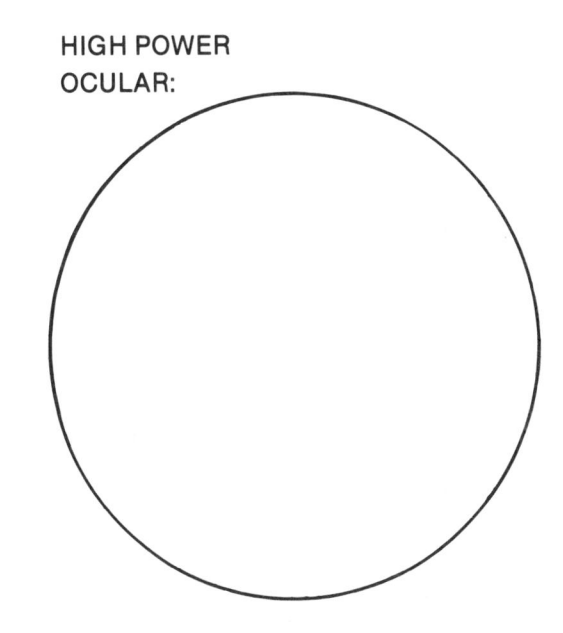

PLANETARY NEBULA
OBSERVATION SHEET

NGC/IC NO.:

DATE: TIME: SEEING(1-10):

TELESCOPE: OCULAR(S):

Questions to be answered in "Description."
1) Is this planetary easy or difficult to identify in your field?
2) What is the overall shape?
3) What is the color of this planetary?
4) Is a disk seen?
5) Are the edges of the disk sharp or diffuse?
6) Is the center brighter, darker or the same brightness as the edge?
7) Are there any other deep-sky objects in the field? If so, what are their names?

DESCRIPTION:

FIELD DRAWING AND NOTES
FINDER FIELD:

LOW POWER
OCULAR:

HIGH POWER
OCULAR:

MORE NOTES:

A BEGINNERS GUIDE TO PLANETARY NEBULAE

It is estimated that our galaxy contains some 50,000 planetary nebulae. Of these, a little more than 1,000 are known to exist. Out of these 1,000 planetaries the *Skalnate Pleso Atlas of the Heavens* lists 144, many of which are suitable for amateur sized instruments. The majority of these 144 planetaries were discovered visually by both William and John Herschel. Today, many writers attribute the term "planetary nebulae" to William Herschel. In 1785, he did mention that most of these objects appeared as a small, hazy greenish disk, not unlike the planet Uranus. However, further research reveals that in 1779, six years before William Herschel's observations, Antione Darquier discovered NGC 6720 (M57). He called his object "perfectly outlined, as large as Jupiter and looks like a fading planet."

Planetary nebulae are probably observed less by amateurs than are the other types of deep-sky objects. One reason for this is simply that most planetaries are small, with many appearing starlike even in large amateur telescopes. Because of this, many planetaries are rather difficult to locate and identify. Yet, there are quite a few planetaries that can be enjoyed through amateur sized instruments and the amateur should make every effort to seek these objects out.

When we talk about planetary nebulae for the amateur, we are in an area where relatively few amateur contributions have been made. Because the available amateur material is scarce, the amateur tends to ignore these objects, a situation that needs to be corrected. For years, the only extensive amateur work was done by John H. Mallas. Using a 4-inch refractor, he surveyed 118 planetary nebulae which were listed in the *Atlas Coeli Catalog*. Of these, he saw and recorded observations for 46 planetaries. His useful observations were compiled in his *Visual Atlas of Planetary Nebulae*, long out of print. This visual atlas of planetaries was an excellent guide for the amateur, but relatively few amateurs even knew of its existence! Included in his atlas was the "Estimated Minimum Telescope Aperture" (EMTA) required to see that particular object—a very useful piece of information for the amateur. In Table 1, I have included his original list of 46 planetaries, including its estimated minimum telescope apertures. As you can see from this table, he has estimated the largest aperture required to see these planetaries is a 4-inch refractor! This is certainly a list of planetaries that even a beginner with a small telescope can search for and expect success.

In Table 2, you will find another list of planetary nebulae. As with Table

1, this second list is intended for the amateur, but requires a telescope in the 8- to 10-inch range. Since many amateurs today possess larger telescopes than their counterparts of years ago, I felt that a more extensive list of planetaries was needed. This second list is composed from objects listed in the catalog section, with only a few exceptions. Table 3 lists the generally accepted classifications for planetary nebulae.

Most amateurs who request information about planetaries inform me that they have problems in identifying them in their field. After identification of the planetary, locating the proper field of view is the second biggest problem many amateurs face. Let me try to explain a procedure for both locating the proper field and, once found, identifying the planetary nebula. Locating the brighter, larger planetaries is not at all difficult. All one needs is a good star atlas such as the *Skalnate Pleso*, a good telescope with a low power wide field ocular and some sweeping of the sky in the appropriate area...success is imminent! Once the bright planetary is found, the observer can then switch to a higher power and look for any detail which may be present.

It's a different story with faint, small, often illusive planetaries that appear starlike in your field. For these objects we need to do a little more searching and use a few more tools.

Let's start again with a star atlas such as the *Skalnate Pleso Atlas of the Heavens*. Locate the planetary on these charts or on an equivalent atlas. Using a companion star catalog, write down the visual magnitude an size of the object. Now, if the object is starlike or extremely small, we will need to use good photographic star atlas with stars down to the 12th magnitude. Two well known photographic atlases, suitable for the amateur, are the *Photographic Star Atlas* and the *Atlas Stellarium*. These atlases have photographic star magnitudes of 13th and 14th magnitude, respectively. Both atlases are by the well known amateur astrophotographer Hans Vehrenberg and can be obtained from many distributors of books. If you do not own a good photographic star atlas, then try to use the one at a planetarium, observatory or university near your home.

Once you have access to a photographic atlas, locate the planetary nebula. Usually a magnifying glass can be very useful when trying to pick out a small disk among the countless stars. Be sure to check and double check until you are certain you have identified the planetary nebula on the photographic star atlas. Make photo copy of this chart, being sure to include a bright star that can be identified on your other star atlas, such as your *Skalnate Pleso*....this is important. You must be able to go from your star atlas directly to the photographic star atlas and not get lost! Go back to your copy of the photographic star atlas and circle your planetary. I usually circle the object on the *back* of the copy sheet and when I use my flashlight from behind, I can see the circle on the photo copy. Now we're all set.

Using your first atlas, identify a bright star or stars near the object. Try to place the planetary between two naked-eye stars and continue as we normally do with the sky comparison method. Another useful method is to star hop from a bright star, identified in the star atlas, to a visible star "near" the object. Whatever method you choose, the end result is the same: Finding a star visible to the naked eye or binoculars that is relatively near our object.

Once this star is found, use a low power wide field ocular and center this star in your telescope's field. Now pick up the photo copy you made of the photographic star atlas. Find, using your photo copy, the path you want to take from the guide star (centered in your field) to planetary. Star hop from this guide star to the planetary. It does require patience but after doing it a few times it becomes rather easy. Once you have located what you believe is the planetary, switch to a higher power to confirm it.

Of course, switching to a higher power does not always help...what then? I have found the use of a small high quality diffraction grating a most valuable aid in identifying starlike planetaries. Take a small square of diffraction grating and place it in a 35mm cardboard slide mount. Place this grating between your eye and the eyepiece. By tilting it slightly on the horizontal axis (with respect to the ocular) you will see that the stars produce a small but obvious spectrum. But the planetary nebula just produces an exact copy of itself... no spectrum. By rotating the diffraction grating you can "see" this extra "star" and follow it back to its source...the planetary nebula! The duplicate "star" that the planetary nebula produces is seen to rotate around the original. At the center of the "circle" produced by the "star" lies the original object, the sought after but starlike planetary nebula...success!

Most of the planetary nebulae listed in Table 2 should not be too difficult for the amateur to locate and identify. The remaining few, those under 20 seconds of arc in size, may not be as easy to identify. For these more illusive but not starlike objects, wait until you have an opportunity to use a large aperture scope such as at a star party. With this larger scope and with the help of another amateur, if necessary, locate and identify the planetary nebula in question. If possible locate the same field through your telescope and attempt to identify the planetary. If you cannot set both telescopes up side by side and compare the same field as seen through both scopes... then make a field drawing through the larger scope. This drawing can be compared with the same field in your smaller scope at a later date. Using this, known as the "Field Comparison Method," you will be surprised at what you can see through your telescope as well as knowing where to look and what to look for. The field comparison method can be used for finding any type of deep-sky object but works especially well on planetary nebulae.

You will also notice an observing form for planetary nebulae. This form contains many of the useful questions that need to be answered while observing planetaries. A similar form can be used for other types of deep-sky objects but different questions should be used. Use this form as a guide only and revise it to suit your particular needs or program.

SELECTED OBJECTS

Here is a list of selected objects which were chosen from among the objects listed in this catalog. You will find these selected objects catagorized as to Object Type, eg: Galaxies, Open Clusters, Planetary Nebulae, Bright Nebulae, Globular Clusters and Dark Nebulae. These objects are not necessarily the brightest or most obvious of each class, but were otherwise considered impressive or interesting to observe.

Omega Centauri NGC 5139

SELECTED OBJECTS

NAME NGC (IC**)		MAGNITUDE	SIZE	CONSTELLATION
GALAXIES:				
55		7.8p	25.0 x 3.0m	Sculptor
247		9.5p	18.2 x 4.5m	Cetus
253		8.9v	24.6 x 4.5m	Sculptor
891		10.9p	11.8 x 1.1m	Andromeda
2903		9.1v	11.0 x 4.6m	Leo
4038		11.0p	2.5 x 2.5m	Corvus
4244		11.9v	14.5 x 1.0m	Canes Venatici
4565		10.2v	14.4 x 1.2m	Coma Berenices
5907		11.3v	11.1 x 0.7m	Draco
PLANETARY NEBULAE:				
246		8.5n/11.3st	240 x 210 s	Cetus
2371-2		13.0n/13.3st	54 x 35 s	Gemini
2392	Eskimo	8.3n/10.5st	47 x 43 s	Gemini
2438		11.3n/16.8st	68 s	Puppis
2440		11.7n/16.5st	54 x 20 s	Puppis
3132	Eight-Burst	8.2n/10.6st	84 x 53 s	Antlia
3242	Ghost/Jupiter	9.0n/11.4st	40 x 35 s	Hydra
6072		14.1n/17.5st	50 x 30 s	Scorpius
6369	Little Ghost	9.9n/16.6st	28 s	Ophiuchus
6818	Little Gem	9.9n/15.0st	22 x 15 s	Sagittarius
6826	Blinking Pl.	8.8n/10.8st	27 x 24 s	Cygnus
7009	Saturn	8.4n/11.7st	44 x 26 s	Aquarius
7293	Helix	6.5n/13.3st	900 x 720 s	Aquarius
7662	Blue Snowball	8.9n/12.5st	32 x 28 s	Andromeda
BRIGHT NEBULAE:				
349**	Merope	4.2st	30.0 x 30.0m	Taurus
206		Bright Knot	—	Andromeda (inv. in M31)
604		Bright Knot	—	Triangulum (inv. in M33)
1491		11.0st	3.0 x 3.0m	Perseus
1579		12.0st	12.0 x 8.0m	Perseus
2023		7.8st	10.0 x 10.0m	Orion
2174-5		7.4st	29.0 x 25.0m	Orion
2237-9	Rosette	—	64.0 x 61.0m	Monoceros
2467		8.5st	4.0 x 4.0m	Puppis
6960	Veil	—	70.0 x 6.0m	Cygnus
6992-5	Veil	—	78.0 x 8.0m	Cygnus
OPEN CLUSTERS:				
663	Letter "S"	7.1v	11.0m	Cassiopeia
869		4.4v	36.0m	Perseus
884		4.7v	36.0m	Perseus
1893	Letter "Y"	8.0v	12.0m	Auriga
2360	Opened Box	9.5v	12.0m	Canis Major
2482	Starfish	8.7v	18.0m	Puppis
6124		6.3v	25.0m	Scorpius

NAME NGC (IC**)	MAGNITUDE	SIZE	CONSTELLATION
GLOBULAR CLUSTER:			
288	7.2p	10.0m	Sculptor
3201	7.4p	7.7m	Vela
5139 Omega Cent.	3.7v	23.0m	Centaurus
5986	8.7v	3.7m	Lupus
6356	8.7v	1.7m	Ophiuchus
DARK NEBULAE:			
B86	—	4.5 x 3.0m	Sagittarious (near NGC6520)
B92	—	15.0m	Sagittarious (near M24)
B143	—	30.0m	Aquila (near Gamma Agilae)

TABLE #1

ESTIMATED MINIMUM TELESCOPE APERTURE*
by John H. Mallas

NAME	EMTA*	CONSTELLATION	NAME	EMTA*	CONSTELLATION
NGC 40	2.4"	Cassiopeia	NGC6309	2.4"	Ophiuchus
246	3-1/4	Cetus	6369	4	Ophiuchus
650-1	2.4	Perseus	6445	4	Sagittarius
IC 289	4	Cassiopeia	6543	2.4	Draco
1514	4	Taurus	6572	2.4	Ophiuchus
1535	3	Eridanus	6567*	3-1/2	Sagittarius
IC 418	4	Lepus	6629	3-1/2	Sagittarius
1952	7 x 50 bin.	Taurus	(M57) 6720	2.4	Lyra
2022	4+	Orion	6741	4	Aquila
2371-2	4+	Gemini	6781	4	Aquila
2392	3	Gemini	PK064+05.1*	4	Cygnus
2438	3-1/2+	Puppis	6818	2.4	Sagittarius
2440	3	Puppis	6826	2.4	Cygnus
3132	2.4	Antlia	(M27) 6853	2	Vulpecula
3242	2.4	Hydra	6879*	4	Sagitta
3587	2.4	Ursa Major	6905*	3	Deleph
4361	4	Corvus	7009	2	Aquarius
IC3568	2.4	Camelopardalis	7027*	3	Cygnus
5882	4	Lupus	7048*	3-1/2	Cygnus
IC4593	4	Serpens	7293	4	Aquarius
6153	4	Scorpius	IC1470	4	Cepheus
6210	2.4	Hercules	7635	3	Cassiopeia
IC4634	3	Ophiuchus	7662	2.4	Andromeda

*Not listed in catalog section

NOT LISTED IN CATALOG SECTION

(1950 Epoch)

NAME	R.A.	DECLINATION	MAGNITUDE	SIZE
6567	18h 10.8m	−19.05	11.7n/15.0st	11 x 7s
PK064 + 05.1	19h 32.8m	+30.25	9.6n/10.3st	5s
6879	20h 08.1m	+16.46	12.1n/15.2st	5s
6905	20h 20.2m	+19.57	11.9n/14.2st	44 x 37s
7027	21h 05.1m	+42.02	10.4n/17.1st	18 x 11s
7048	21h 12.6m	+46.04	11.3n/18.3st	60 x 50s

The 16" Casa Grande telescope at Flandreau Planetarium in Tucson, Arizona.

TABLE #2

PLANETARY NEBULAE CLASSIFICATION

VORONSOV-VELJAMINOV:
- I = Stellar
- IIa = Oval, homogeneously bright, concentrated
- IIb = Oval, homogeneously bright, w/o concentration
- IIIa = Oval, unhomogeneously bright
- IIIb = Oval, unhomogeneously bright with brighter edges
- IV = Annular
- V = irregular, intermediate to diffuse nebulosity
- VI = anomal

TABLE #3

PLANETARY NEBULAE FOR THE SMALL TELESCOPE

NGC (IC*)		CONSTELLATION	R.A.	DEC.	MAGNITUDE	SIZE	
40		Cepheus	00h 10.2m	+72.15	10.2n/11.4st	60 x 38s	
246		Cetus	00h 44.6m	−12.09	8.5n/11.3st	240 x 210s	
289*		Cassiopeia	03h 06.2m	+61.08	12.3n/15.0st	45 x 30s	
418*		Lepus	05h 25.4m	−12.44	12.0n/10.9st	14 x 11s	
650-1	(M76)	Perseus	01h 38.8m	+51.19	12.2n/16.6st	157 x 87s	Barbell
1470*		Cepheus	23h 03.2m	+59.59	8.1n/11.9st	70 x 45s	
1501		Camelopardalis	04h 02.6m	+60.47	13.3n/13.4st	56 x 48s	
1514		Taurus	04h 06.1m	+30.38	10.8n/ 9.7st	120 x 90s	
1535		Eridanus	04h 12.1m	−12.52	9.3n/11.8st	20 x 17s	
1952	(M1)	Taurus	05h 31.5m	+21.59	8.4n/15.9st	360 x 240s	Crab
2022		Orion	05h 39.3m	+09.03	12.8n/14.6st	28 x 27s	
2149*		Auriga	05h 52.6m	+46.07	9.9n/14.0st	15 x 10s	
2371-2		Gemini	07h 22.4m	+29.35	13.0n/13.3st	54 x 35s	
2392		Gemini	07h 26.2m	+21.01	8.3n/10.5st	47 x 43s	Eskimo
2438		Puppis	07h 39.6m	−14.36	11.3n/16.8st	68s	
2440		Puppis	07h 39.9m	−18.05	11.7n/16.5st	54 x 20s	
3132		Antlia	10h 04.9m	−40.11	8.2n/10.6st	84 x 53s	Eight-Burst
3242		Hydra	10h 22.4m	−18.23	9.0n/11.4st	40 x 35s	Ghost of Jupiter
3568*		Camelopardalis	12h 32.4m	+82.51	11.6n/12.0st	18s	
3587	(M97)	Ursa Major	11h 12.0m	+55.18	12.0n/14.3st	203 x 199s	Owl
4361		Corvus	12h 21.9m	−18.29	10.8n/12.8st	81s	
4406*		Lupus	14h 19.3m	−43.55	10.6n/—	100 x 37s	
4593*		Serpens	16h 09.5m	+12.12	10.2n/10.2st	15 x 11s	White-Eyed Pea
4634*		Ophiuchus	16h 58.5m	−21.44	12.3n/17.4st	20 x 9s	
6153		Scorpius	16h 28.0m	−40.08	11.5n/—	28 x 21s	
6210		Hercules	16h 42.5m	+23.53	9.7n/12.5st	20 x 13s	
6302**		Scorpius	17h 10.4m	−37.03	11.4n/—	120 x 60s	Bug
6309		Ophiuchus	17h 11.2m	−12.51	11.6n/14.1st	19 x 10s	Box Nebula
6369		Ophiuchus	17h 26.3m	−23.44	9.9n/16.6st	28s	Little Ghost
6445		Sagittarius	17h 46.3m	−20.00	13.2n/19.1st	38 x 29s	Crescent
6543		Draco	17h 58.8m	+66.38	8.8n/11.1st	22s	Cat's Eye
6563		Sagittarius	18h 08.8m	−33.53	13.8n/18.3st	50 x 37s	
6567**		Sagittarius	18h 10.8m	−19.05	11.7n/15.0st	11 x 7s	
6572		Ophiuchus	18h 09.7m	+06.50	9.6n/12.0st	16 x 13s	
6629		Sagittarius	18h 22.7m	−23.14	10.6n/13.6st	16 x 14s	
6720	(M57)	Lyra	18h 51.7m	+32.58	9.3n/14.7st	83 x 59s	Ring
6741		Aquila	19h 00.1m	−00.31	11.7n/16.7st	9 x 7s	Phantom Streak
6751		Aquila	19h 03.2m	−06.05	12.2n/13.3st	21s	
6781		Aquila	19h 16.0m	+06.26	12.5n/15.4st	106s	
6804		Aquila	19h 29.2m	+09.07	13.3n/13.3st	63 x 50s	
6818		Sagittarius	19h 41.4m	−14.17	9.9n/15.0st	22 x 15s	Little Gem
6826		Cygnus	19h 43.4m	+50.24	8.8n/10.8st	27 x 24s	Blinking Pl.
6853	(M27)	Vulpecula	19h 57.4m	+22.35	7.6n/13.4st	480 x 240s	Dumbbell
6891**		Aquila	20h 12.8m	+12.35	11.4n/11.6st	15 x 7s	
6905**		Delephinus	20h 20.2m	+19.57	11.9n/14.2st	44 x 37s	Blue Flash
7008		Cygnus	20h 59.1m	+54.21	13.3n/12.9st	86 x 69s	
7009		Aquarius	21h 01.4m	−11.34	8.4n/11.7st	44 x 26s	Saturn
7027**		Cygnus	21h 05.1m	+42.02	10.4n/17.1st	18 x 11s	
7048		Cygnus	21h 12.6m	+46.04	11.3n/18.3st	60 x 50s	

NGC (IC*)	CONSTELLATION	R.A.	DEC.	MAGNITUDE	SIZE	
7293	Aquarius	22h 27.0m	−21.06	6.5n/13.3st	900 x 720s	Helix
7635	Cassiopeia	23h 18.5m	+60.54	8.5n/ 8.5st	205 x 180s	Bubble
7662	Andromeda	23h 23.5m	+42.14	8.9n/12.5st	32 x 28s	Blue Snowball

**Not listed in catalog section

Both telescopes are homemade by the author. The white telescope is a 6" F6 and the red one is a 10" F5.6.

TABLE #4

TELESCOPES USED IN THE CATALOG SECTION

7 x 50	binoculars		
2.4	inch	F/12	Refractor
6	inch	F/6	Reflector
6	inch	F/8	Reflector
8	inch	F/5	Reflector
8	inch	F/7	Reflector
8	inch	F/8	Reflector
8	inch	F/10	Schmidt-Cassegrain
10	inch	F/5	Reflector
10	inch	F/5.5	Reflector
10	inch	F/5.6	Reflector
10	inch	F/6.1	Reflector
16	inch	F/11	Cassegrain

TABLE #5

MESSIER OBJECTS IN CATALOG

M 1	=	NGC	1952	M38	=	NGC	1912	M75	=	NGC	6864
M 2	=	NGC	7089	M39	=	NGC	7092	M76	=	NGC	650
M 3	=	NGC	5272	M40	=	NGC	Winnecke 4	M77	=	NGC	1068
M 4	=	NGC	6121	M41	=	NGC	2287	M78	=	NGC	2068
M 5	=	NGC	5904	M42	=	NGC	1976	M79	=	NGC	1904
M 6	=	NGC	6405	M43	=	NGC	1982	M80	=	NGC	6093
M 7	=	NGC	6475	M44	=	NGC	2632	M81	=	NGC	3031
M 8	=	NGC	6523	M45	=	NGC	Mel 22	M82	=	NGC	3034
M 9	=	NGC	6333	M46	=	NGC	2437	M83	=	NGC	5236
M10	=	NGC	6254	M47	=	NGC	2422	M84	=	NGC	4374
M11	=	NGC	6705	M48	=	NGC	2548	M85	=	NGC	4382
M12	=	NGC	6218	M49	=	NGC	4472	M86	=	NGC	4406
M13	=	NGC	6205	M50	=	NGC	2323	M87	=	NGC	4486
M14	=	NGC	6402	M51	=	NGC	5194	M88	=	NGC	4501
M15	=	NGC	7078	M52	=	NGC	7654	M89	=	NGC	4552
M16	=	NGC	6611	M53	=	NGC	5024	M90	=	NGC	4569
M17	=	NGC	6618	M54	=	NGC	6715	M91	=	NGC	4548
M18	=	NGC	6613	M55	=	NGC	6809	M92	=	NGC	6341
M19	=	NGC	6273	M56	=	NGC	6779	M93	=	NGC	2447
M20	=	NGC	6514	M57	=	NGC	6720	M94	=	NGC	4736
M21	=	NGC	6531	M58	=	NGC	4579	M95	=	NGC	3351
M22	=	NGC	6656	M59	=	NGC	4621	M96	=	NGC	3368
M23	=	NGC	6494	M60	=	NGC	4649	M97	=	NGC	3587
M24	=	NGC	6603	M61	=	NGC	4303	M98	=	NGC	4192
M25	=	I.C.	4725	M62	=	NGC	6266	M99	=	NGC	4254
M26	=	NGC	6694	M63	=	NGC	5055	M100	=	NGC	4321
M27	=	NGC	6853	M64	=	NGC	4826	M101	=	NGC	5457
M28	=	NGC	6626	M65	=	NGC	3623	M102	=	NGC	5866
M29	=	NGC	6913	M66	=	NGC	3627	M103	=	NGC	581
M30	=	NGC	7099	M67	=	NGC	2682	M104	=	NGC	4594
M31	=	NGC	224	M68	=	NGC	4590	M105	=	NGC	3379
M32	=	NGC	221	M69	=	NGC	6637	M106	=	NGC	4258
M33	=	NGC	598	M70	=	NGC	6681	M107	=	NGC	6171
M34	=	NGC	1039	M71	=	NGC	6838	M108	=	NGC	3556
M35	=	NGC	2168	M72	=	NGC	6981	M109	=	NGC	3992
M36	=	NGC	1960	M73	=	NGC	6994	M110	=	NGC	205
M37	=	NGC	2099	M74	=	NGC	628				

TABLE #6

OBJECTS LISTED IN THE CATALOG

NAME		TYPE	MAGNITUDE	SIZE	R.A.	DEC.	COMMENTS
NGC	40	Pl.Nb.	10.2n/11.4st	60.0 x 38.0 s	00h 10.2m	+72.15	
	45	Gal.	12.1p	8.0 x 5.5m	00h 11.4m	−23.27	
	55	Gal.	7.8p	25.0 x 3.0m	00h 12.5m	−39.30	
	185	Gal.	11.7v	2.2 x 2.2m	00h 36.1m	+48.04	
	205	Gal.	9.4v	10.0 x 4.5m	00h 37.6m	+41.25	
	206	Bt.Kt.	—	—	—	—	Inv. in 224
	221	Gal.	8.7v	3.4 x 2.8m	00h 40.0m	+40.36	
	224	Gal.	4.8v	160.1 x 35.0m	00h 40.0m	+41.00	
	246	Pl.Nb.	8.5n/11.3st	240.0 x 210.0 s	00h 44.6m	−12.09	
	247	Gal.	9.5p	18.2 x 4.5m	00h 44.6m	−21.01	
	253	Gal.	8.9v	24.6 x 4.5m	00h 45.1m	−25.34	
	255	Gal.	12.4p	3.3 x 2.5m	00h 45.2m	−11.45	
	281	B.N.	8.6st	27.0 x 23.0m	00h 50.4m	+56.19	
	288	Gb.	7.2p	10.0m	00h 50.2m	−26.52	
	300	Gal.	11.3p	20.0 x 10.0m	00h 52.6m	−37.58	
	404	Gal.	10.7v	2.1 x 2.0m	01h 06.6m	+35.27	
	428	Gal.	11.7p	3.9 x 3.6m	01h 10.4m	+00.43	
	488	Gal.	11.1v	4.2 x 3.3m	01h 19.1m	+05.00	
	524	Gal.	11.1v	1.8 x 1.7m	01h 22.1m	+09.16	
	581	Cl.	7.4v	5.0m	01h 29.9m	+60.27	About 60 st
	598	Gal.	6.7v	65.0 x 35.0m	01h 31.1m	+30.24	
	604	Bt.Kt.	—	—	—	—	Inv. in 598
	628	Gal	10.2v	10.6 x 9.0m	01h 34.0m	+15.32	
	650-1	Pl.Nb.	12.2n/16.6st	157.0 x 87.0 s	01h 38.8m	+51.19	
	654	Cl.	9.1v	5.0m	01h 40.5m	+61.39	About 50 st
	659	Cl.	9.8v	5.0m	01h 40.8m	+60.28	About 30 st
	663	Cl.	7.1v	11.0m	01h 42.6m	+61.01	About 80 st
	670	Gal.	13.0p	0.9 x 0.5m	01h 44.5m	+27.38	
	672	Gal	12.2v	5.5 x 1.5m	01h 45.0m	+27.11	
	736	Gal.	13.6p	—	01h 53.8m	+32.48	Not in S.P.
	750-1	Gal.	13.7p	0.6 x 0.3m	01h 54.6m	+32.58	
	752	Cl.	7.0v	45.0m	01h 54.7m	+37.25	About 70 st
	772	Gal.	10.9v	5.0 x 3.0m	01h 56.6m	+18.46	
	777	Gal.	13.0p	0.9 x 0.7m	01h 57.3m	+31.12	
	783	Gal.	12.8p	—	01h 58.2m	+31.38	Not in S.P.
	784	Gal.	12.1p	—	01h 58.4m	+28.35	Not in S.P.
	812	Gal.	12.8p	—	02h 03.7m	+44.20	Not in S.P.
	846	Gal.	13.2p	—	02h 09.7m	+44.20	Not in S.P.
	869	Cl.	4.4v	36.0m	02h 15.5m	+56.55	About 350 st
	884	Cl.	4.7v	36.0m	02h 18.9m	+56.53	About 300 st
	890	Gal.	12.6p	1.1 x 0.7m	02h 19.1m	+33.02	
	891	Gal.	10.9p	11.8 x 1.1m	02h 19.3m	+42.07	
	925	Gal.	10.5p	9.5 x 4.3m	02h 24.3m	+33.22	
	936	Gal.	10.7v	3.3 x 2.5m	02h 25.1m	−01.22	
	949	Gal.	12.7v	1.2 x 0.5m	02h 27.6m	+36.56	
	1023	Gal.	10.5p	4.0 x 1.2m	02h 37.2m	+38.52	
	1032	Gal.	13.2p	—	02h 36.8m	+00.53	Not in S.P.
	1035	Gal.	12.8p	1.9 x 0.6m	02h 37.0m	−08.20	
	1039	Cl.	5.5v	18.0m	02h 38.8m	+42.34	About 80 st
	1048	Gal.	12.5p	4.5 x 2.6m	02h 38.2m	−08.45	

NAME		TYPE	MAGNITUDE	SIZE	R.A.	DEC.	COMMENTS
NGC	1052	Gal.	11.2v	1.3 x 1.0m	02h 38.6m	−08.28	
	1055	Gal.	11.4p	6.7 x 1.5m	02h 39.2m	+00.16	
	1058	Gal.	11.7p	2.3 x 2.1m	02h 40.2m	+37.08	
	1068	Gal.	8.9v	6.0 x 5.0m	02h 40.1m	−00.14	
	1073	Gal.	11.4p	4.5 x 4.2m	02h 41.2m	+01.10	
	1087	Gal.	11.9v	2.2 x 1.2m	02h 43.9m	−00.42	
	1090	Gal.	12.5p	2.8 x 1.0m	02h 44.0m	−00.27	
	1094	Gal.	13.5p	—	02h 44.9m	−00.30	Not in S.P.
	1097	Gal.	10.6p	9.0 x 5.5m	02h 44.3m	−30.29	
	1232	Gal.	12.5p	7.0 x 5.5m	03h 07.5m	−20.46	
	1316	Gal.	10.1p	3.5 x 2.5m	03h 20.7m	−37.25	
	1317	Gal.	12.2p	0.7 x 0.6m	03h 20.8m	−37.17	
	1332	Gal.	10.4v	3.4 x 1.0m	03h 24.1m	−21.31	
	1365	Gal.	11.2p	8.0 x 3.5m	03h 31.8m	−36.18	
	1374	Gal.	12.4p	0.8 x 0.8m	03h 33.4m	−35.24	
	1379	Gal.	12.3p	0.6 x 0.6m	03h 34.2m	−35.37	
	1380	Gal.	11.4p	3.0 x 1.0m	03h 34.6m	−35.09	
	1381	Gal.	12.6p	2.0 x 0.5m	03h 34.7m	−35.28	
	1386	Gal.	12.4p	2.5 x 1.0m	03h 35.0m	−36.10	
	1387	Gal.	12.1p	1.0 x 0.9m	03h 35.1m	−35.41	
	1389	Gal.	12.8p	1.0 x 0.8m	03h 35.3m	−35.55	
	1399	Gal.	10.9p	1.4 x 1.4m	03h 36.6m	−35.37	
	1404	Gal.	11.5p	1.0 x 1.0m	03h 37.0m	−35.45	
	1427	Gal.	12.4p	—	03h 40.4m	−35.34	
	1437	Gal.	12.9p	2.0 x 1.5m	03h 41.7m	−36.01	
	1491	B.N.	11.0st	3.0 x 3.0m	03h 59.5m	+51.10	
	1501	Pl.Nb.	13.3n/13.4st	56.0 x 48.0 s	04h 02.6m	+60.47	
	1502	Cl.	5.3v	7.0m	04h 03.0m	+26.11	About 15 st
	1514	Pl.Nb.	10.8n/9.7st	120.0 x 90.0 s	04h 06.1m	+30.38	
	1535	Pl.Nb.	9.3n/11.8st	20.0 x 17.0 s	04h 12.1m	−12.52	
	1579	B.N.	12.0st	12.0 x 8.0m	04h 26.9m	+35.10	
	1625	Gal.	13.1p	1.8 x 0.3m	04h 34.6m	−03.24	
	1637	Gal.	12.1v	2.6 x 1.9m	04h 38.9m	−20.56	
	1638	Gal.	13.1p	0.6 x 0.5m	04h 39.1m	−01.53	
	1647	Cl.	6.3v	40.0m	04h 43.2m	+18.59	About 30 st
	1720	Gal.	13.0p	—	04h 57.7m	−07.53	Not in S.P.
	1726	Gal.	13.0p	0.6 x 0.5m	04h 57.3m	−07.49	
	1746	Cl.	6.0v	45.0m	05h 00.6m	+23.44	About 60 st
	1784	Gal.	12.4p	4.5 x 2.3m	05h 03.2m	−11.56	
	1792	Gal.	10.7p	3.0 x 1.0m	05h 03.5m	−38.04	
	1807	Cl.	7.8v	10.0m	05h 07.8m	+16.28	About 15 st
	1808	Gal.	11.2p	4.0 x 1.0m	05h 05.9m	−37.34	
	1817	Cl.	7.9v	15.0m	05h 09.2m	+16.38	About 10 st
	1851	Gb.	8.1v	5.3m	05h 12.4m	−40.05	
	1893	Cl.	8.0v	12.0m	05h 22.4m	+33.21	About 20 st
	1904	Gb.	8.4v	3.2m	05h 22.2m	−24.34	
	1907	Cl.	9.9v	5.0m	05h 24.7m	+35.17	About 40 st
	1912	Cl.	7.4v	20.0m	05h 25.3m	+35.48	About 100 st
	1931	B.N.	—	3.0 x 3.0m	05h 28.1m	+34.13	
	1952	Pl.Nb.	8.4n/15.9st	360.0 x 240.0 s	05h 31.5m	+21.59	
	1960	Cl.	6.3v	12.0m	05h 32.0m	+34.07	About 60 st
	1964	Gal.	11.6p	5.4 x 1.1m	05h 31.2m	−21.59	
	1976	B.N.	—	66.0 x 60.0m	05h 32.9m	−05.25	
	1982	B.N.	9.1st	20.0 x 15.0m	05h 33.1m	−05.18	
	1999	B.N.	9.5st	16.0 x 12.0m	05h 34.1m	−06.45	

NAME		TYPE	MAGNITUDE	SIZE	R.A.	DEC.	COMMENTS
NGC	2022	Pl.Nb.	12.8n/14.6st	28.0 x 27.0 s	05h 39.3m	+09.03	
	2023	B.N.	7.8st	10.0 x 10.0m	05h 39.2m	−02.15	
	2024	B.N.	01.9st	30.0 x 30.0m	05h 39.4m	−01.52	
	2068	B.N.	10.3st	8.0 x 6.0m	05h 44.2m	+00.02	
	2090	Gal.	12.4p	2.5 x 1.0m	05h 45.2m	−34.15	
	2099	Cl.	6.2v	20.0m	05h 49.0m	+32.33	About 150 st
	2126	Cl.	9.8v	6.5m	05h 58.1m	+49.55	About 28 st
	2139	Gal.	11.9p	1.6 x 1.3m	05h 58.6m	+23.49	
	2146	Gal.	11.3p	5.1 x 2.8m	06h 10.7m	+78.23	
	2158	Cl.	12.5v	4.0m	06h 04.3m	+24.06	About 40 st
	2168	Cl.	5.3v	40.0m	06h 05.7m	+24.20	About 120 st
	2169	Cl.	6.4v	5.0m	06h 05.7m	+13.58	About 18 st
	2174-5	B.N.	7.4st	29.0 x 25.0m	06h 06.7m	+20.31	
	2194	Cl.	9.2v	8.0m	06h 11.0m	+12.50	About 100 st
	2196	Gal.	12.6p	1.7 x 1.3m	06h 10.1m	−21.47	
	2207	Gal.	11.4p	2.8 x 1.9m	06h 14.3m	−21.21	
	2217	Gal.	11.8p	5.0 x 4.0m	06h 18.7m	−27.14	
	2237-9	B.N.	—	64.0 x 61.0m	06h 29.6m	+04.40	
	2244	Cl.	6.2v	40.0m	06h 29.7m	+04.54	About 16 st
	2250	Cl.	9.0v	—	06h 31.5m	−05.01	Not in S.P.
	2252	Cl.	7.5v	—	06h 33.6m	+05.24	Not in S.P.
	2261	B.N.	var.	var.	06h 36.4m	+08.46	Hubbles Var.
	2268	Gal.	12.2p	2.3 x 1.5m	07h 01.3m	+84.30	
	2276	Gal.	12.9p	2.2 x 1.9m	07h 11.0m	+85.52	
	2280	Gal.	12.7p	2.0 x 1.0m	06h 42.8m	−27.35	
	2287	Cl.	5.0v	30.0m	07h 44.9m	−20.42	About 50 st
	2300	Gal.	12.2p	1.0 x 0.9m	07h 16.5m	+85.50	
	2323	Cl.	6.9v	16.0m	07h 00.5m	−08.16	About 100 st
	2325	Gal.	12.9p	—	07h 00.7m	−28.38	
	2336	Gal.	11.0p	5.7 x 2.8m	07h 16.2m	+80.20	
	2339	Gal.	12.5v	2.1 x 1.3m	07h 05.4m	+18.52	
	2360	Cl.	9.5v	12.0m	07h 15.4m	−15.33	About 50 st
	2362	Cl.	10.5v	6.0m	07h 16.6m	−24.52	About 40 st
	2371-2	Pl.Nb.	13.0n/13.3st	54.0 x 35.0 s	07h 22.4m	+29.35	
	2392	Pl.Nb.	8.3n/10.5st	47.0 x 43.0 s	07h 26.2m	+21.01	
	2403	Gal.	8.9v	16.8 x 10.0m	07h 32.0m	+65.43	
	2422	Cl.	4.5v	25.0m	07h 34.3m	−14.22	About 50 st
	2423	Cl.	6.9v	20.0m	07h 34.8m	−13.45	About 60 st
	2425	Cl.	—	—	07h 31.1m	−14.48	Not in S.P.
	2437	Cl.	6.0v	24.0m	07h 39.6m	−14.42	About 150 st
	2438	Pl.Nb.	11.3n/16.8st	68.0 s	07h 39.6m	−14.36	
	2440	Pl.Nb.	11.7n/16.5st	54.0 x 20.0 s	07h 39.9m	−18.05	
	2447	Cl.	6.0v	25.0m	07h 42.4m	−23.45	About 60 st
	2452	Pl.Nb.	12.6n/19.0st	22.0 x 16.0 s	07h 45.6m	−27.13	
	2453	Cl.	9.4v	5.0m	07h 45.7m	−27.07	About 20 st
	2467	B.N.	8.5st	4.0 x 4.0m	07h 51.3m	−26.16	
	2477	Cl.	5.7v	25.0m	07h 50.5m	−38.25	About 300 st
	2482	Cl.	8.7v	18.0m	07h 52.8m	−24.10	About 50 st
	2547	Cl.	5.1v	15.0m	08h 08.9m	−49.07	About 50 st
	2548	Cl.	5.3v	30.0m	08h 11.2m	−05.38	About 80 st
	2632	Cl.	3.7v	95.0m	08h 37.5m	+19.52	About 75 st
	2655	Gal.	10.7v	5.0 x 3.4m	08h 49.4m	+78.25	
	2672	Gal.	12.2v	0.8 x 0.7m	08h 46.6m	+19.16	
	2681	Gal.	10.4v	2.8 x 2.5m	08h 50.0m	+51.31	
	2682	Cl.	6.1v	15.0m	08h 48.3m	+12.00	About 65 st

NAME		TYPE	MAGNITUDE	SIZE	R.A.	DEC.	COMMENTS
NGC	2683	Gal.	9.6v	8.0 x 1.3m	08h 49.6m	+33.38	
	2715	Gal.	11.9v	4.4 x 1.1m	09h 02.0m	+78.16	
	2748	Gal.	11.4v	2.3 x 0.8m	09h 08.2m	+76.41	
	2763	Gal.	12.6p	1.7 x 1.7m	09h 04.5m	−15.17	
	2775	Gal.	10.7v	2.3 x 1.9m	09h 07.7m	+07.15	
	2781	Gal.	11.7v	3.2 x 1.3m	09h 09.1m	−14.36	
	2784	Gal.	11.8p	3.0 x 1.1m	09h 10.1m	−23.58	
	2792	Pl.Nb.	13.5n	13.0 s	09h 10.6m	−42.14	
	2811	Gal.	11.7v	1.6 x 0.5m	09h 13.9m	−16.06	
	2815	Gal.	12.9p	3.0 x 0.7m	09h 14.1m	−23.24	
	2832	Gal.	13.5p	0.6 x 0.6m	09h 16.8m	+33.59	
	2835	Gal.	12.0p	5.8 x 2.8m	09h 15.7m	−22.08	
	2841	Gal.	9.3v	6.4 x 2.4m	09h 18.6m	+51.12	
	2848	Gal.	12.8p	2.1 x 1.4m	09h 17.8m	−16.18	
	2855	Gal.	12.2v	1.1 x 1.0m	09h 19.1m	−11.41	
	2859	Gal.	10.7v	4.4 x 3.5m	09h 21.3m	+34.44	
	2865	Gal.	12.5p	0.8 x 0.5m	09h 21.2m	−22.58	
	2889	Gal.	12.4p	1.3 x 1.2m	09h 24.8m	−11.25	
	2903	Gal.	9.1v	11.0 x 4.6m	09h 29.3m	+21.44	
	2964	Gal.	11.0v	2.2 x 1.1m	09h 40.0m	+32.05	
	2968	Gal.	11.9v	1.2 x 0.8m	09h 40.3m	+32.10	
	2974	Gal.	11.0v	1.5 x 0.9m	09h 40.0m	−03.29	
	2992	Gal.	13.0p	—	09h 43.3m	−14.06	
	2993	Gal.	13.0p	—	09h 43.3m	−14.08	
	2997	Gal.	11.0p	6.0 x 5.0m	09h 43.5m	−30.58	
	3003	Gal.	12.7v	5.0 x 0.9m	09h 45.6m	+33.39	
	3021	Gal.	11.7v	1.0 x 0.5m	09h 48.0m	+33.47	
	3031	Gal.	7.9v	21.0 x 9.8m	09h 51.5m	+69.18	
	3034	Gal.	8.8v	9.0 x 4.0m	09h 51.9m	+69.56	
	3044	Gal.	12.6p	4.6 x 0.5m	09h 51.0m	+01.49	
	3054	Gal.	12.6p	3.3 x 1.3m	09h 52.1m	−25.28	
	3079	Gal.	11.2v	8.0 x 1.0m	09h 58.6m	+55.57	
	3109	Gal.	11.2p	12.0 x 2.0m	10h 00.8m	−25.55	
	3115	Gal.	9.3v	4.0 x 1.2m	10h 02.8m	−07.28	
	3132	Pl.Nb.	8.2n/10.6st	84.0 x 53.0 s	10h 04.9m	−40.11	
	3158	Gal.	13.1p	0.6 x 0.5m	10h 10.9m	+39.00	
	3162	Gal.	12.3p	2.3 x 2.1m	10h 10.7m	+22.59	
	3166	Gal.	11.4v	4.4 x 1.7m	10h 11.2m	+03.40	
	3169	Gal.	11.7v	4.0 x 1.7m	10h 11.7m	+03.43	
	3172	Gal.	14.9p	—	10h 14.6m	+89.14	Not in S.P.
	3177	Gal.	12.8p	0.8 x 0.7m	10h 13.9m	+21.22	
	3184	Gal.	9.6v	5.6 x 5.6m	10h 15.2m	+41.40	
	3185	Gal.	12.9p	1.4 x 0.9m	10h 14.9m	+21.56	
	3187	Gal.	13.0v	—	10h 16.4m	+21.59	Not in S.P.
	3190	Gal.	11.3v	3.0 x 1.0m	10h 15.4m	+22.05	
	3193	Gal.	11.5v	0.9 x 0.9m	10h 15.7m	+22.09	
	3201	Gb.	7.4p	7.7m	10h 15.5m	−46.09	
	3213	Gal.	14.3p	—	10h 20.0m	+19.46	Not in S.P.
	3222	Gal.	14.5p	—	10h 21.2m	+20.00	Not in S.P.
	3226	Gal.	11.4v	1.0 x 0.8m	10h 20.7m	+20.09	
	3227	Gal.	11.4v	3.0 x 1.2m	10h 20.7m	+20.07	
	3242	Pl.Nb.	9.0n/11.4st	40.0 x 35.0 s	10h 22.4m	−18.23	
	3245	Gal.	11.2v	1.8 x 0.9m	10h 24.5m	+28.46	
	3254	Gal.	12.2v	4.0 x 1.0m	10h 26.5m	+29.45	
	3277	Gal.	12.0v	1.1 x 0.9m	10h 30.2m	+28.46	

NAME		TYPE	MAGNITUDE	SIZE	R.A.	DEC.	COMMENTS
NGC	3294	Gal.	11.4v	2.6 x 1.2m	10h 33.4m	+37.35	
	3338	Gal.	11.3p	4.5 x 3.0m	10h 39.5m	+14.00	
	3344	Gal.	10.4v	7.6 x 6.2m	10h 40.7m	+25.11	
	3346	Gal.	11.7v	2.2 x 2.0m	10h 41.0m	+15.09	
	3351	Gal.	10.4v	6.1 x 3.9m	10h 41.3m	+11.58	
	3367	Gal.	11.9p	1.9 x 1.7m	10h 44.0m	+14.01	
	3368	Gal.	9.1v	5.0 x 4.0m	10h 44.2m	+12.05	
	3377	Gal.	10.5v	1.9 x 1.0m	10h 45.1m	+14.15	
	3379	Gal.	9.2v	2.2 x 2.0m	10h 45.2m	+12.51	
	3384	Gal.	10.2v	4.4 x 1.4m	10h 45.7m	+12.54	
	3389	Gal.	12.5v	2.3 x 1.0m	10h 45.8m	+12.48	
	3395	Gal.	12.0v	1.5 x 0.9m	10h 47.1m	+33.15	
	3396	Gal.	12.7v	0.8m	10h 47.2m	+33.16	
	3412	Gal.	10.4v	2.4 x 1.1m	10h 48.3m	+13.41	
	3413	Gal.	13.0p	—	10h 50.0m	+32.34	Not in S.P.
	3414	Gal.	11.0v	1.4 x 1.0m	10h 48.6m	+28.15	
	3423	Gal.	11.5p	3.5 x 2.8m	10h 48.7m	+06.07	
	3424	Gal.	13.2p	—	10h 50.4m	+33.02	Not in S.P.
	3430	Gal.	12.0v	3.4 x 2.0m	10h 49.5m	+33.14	
	3432	Gal.	11.4v	5.8 x 0.8m	10h 49.7m	+36.54	
	3442	Gal.	13.0p	—	10h 51.7m	+34.02	Not in S.P.
	3486	Gal.	11.2v	6.8 x 4.5m	10h 57.8m	+29.15	
	3504	Gal.	10.9v	2.2 x 2.2m	11h 00.5m	+28.15	
	3511	Gal.	11.9p	4.6 x 2.0m	11h 00.8m	−22.50	
	3512	Gal.	11.7v	1.2 x 1.0m	11h 01.3m	+28.18	
	3513	Gal.	12.0p	1.9 x 1.3m	11h 01.1m	−22.58	
	3556	Gal.	10.7v	7.7 x 1.3m	11h 08.7m	+55.57	
	3587	Pl.Nb.	12.0n/14.3st	203.0 x 199.0 s	11h 12.0m	+55.18	
	3593	Gal.	11.3v	2.5 x 0.9m	11h 12.0m	+13.06	
	3623	Gal.	9.3v	7.8 x 1.5m	11h 16.3m	+13.23	
	3627	Gal.	8.4v	8.0 x 2.5m	11h 17.6m	+13.17	
	3628	Gal.	10.9v	12.0 x 1.5m	11h 17.7m	+13.53	
	3640	Gal.	10.7v	1.1 x 1.0m	11h 18.5m	+03.31	
	3681	Gal.	12.4v	1.0 x 0.9m	11h 23.9m	+17.09	
	3684	Gal.	12.4v	2.8 x 1.8m	11h 24.5m	+17.18	
	3686	Gal.	11.4v	2.4 x 1.8m	11h 25.1m	+17.30	
	3726	Gal.	10.8p	5.7 x 3.4m	11h 30.7m	+47.19	
	3782	Gal.	12.9p	1.2 x 0.7m	11h 36.9m	+46.44	
	3877	Gal.	10.9v	4.4 x 0.8m	11h 43.5m	+47.46	
	3893	Gal.	11.3v	3.7 x 1.9m	11h 46.1m	+49.00	
	3896	Gal.	14.0p	—	11h 47.6m	+48.49	Not in S.P.
	3949	Gal.	11.0v	2.3 x 1.1m	11h 51.1m	+48.08	
	3976	Gal.	12.4p	3.3 x 0.8m	11h 53.4m	+07.02	
	3981	Gal.	12.7p	3.2 x 1.3m	11h 53.7m	−19.37	
	3985	Gal.	12.9p	0.9 x 0.6m	11h 54.1m	+48.37	
	3992	Gal.	10.8v	6.2 x 3.5m	11h 55.0m	+53.39	
	4027	Gal.	11.6p	2.4 x 2.0m	11h 57.0m	−18.59	
	4030	Gal.	11.0v	3.1 x 2.2m	11h 57.8m	−00.49	
	4038	Gal.	11.0p	2.5 x 2.5m	11h 59.3m	−18.35	
	4045	Gal.	12.8p	1.2 x 1.0m	12h 00.2m	+02.15	
	4100	Gal.	11.9v	5.0 x 1.2m	12h 03.6m	+49.51	
	4116	Gal.	12.3p	3.1 x 1.2m	12h 05.1m	+02.58	
	4123	Gal.	11.8p	3.2 x 2.0m	12h 05.6m	+03.09	
	4144	Gal.	12.4p	5.2 x 0.7m	12h 07.5m	+46.44	
	4147	Gb.	9.4v	1.7m	12h 07.6m	+18.49	

NAME		TYPE	MAGNITUDE	SIZE		R.A.	DEC.	COMMENTS
NGC	4151	Gal.	11.6v	2.5 x	1.6m	12h 08.0m	+39.41	
	4190	Gal.	13.2p	1.1 x	0.8m	12h 11.1m	+36.54	
	4192	Gal.	10.7v	8.4 x	1.9m	12h 11.3m	+15.11	
	4203	Gal.	11.0v	1.8 x	1.5m	12h 12.5m	+33.29	
	4214	Gal.	10.3v	6.6 x	5.8m	12h 30.1m	+36.36	
	4215	Gal.	12.8p	1.1 x	0.4m	12h 13.4m	+06.41	
	4217	Gal.	11.9p	4.5 x	0.9m	12h 13.3m	+47.22	
	4220	Gal.	11.7v	2.6 x	0.8m	12h 13.7m	+48.10	
	4224	Gal.	12.9p	1.5 x	0.6m	12h 14.0m	+07.44	
	4226	Gal.	14.4p	—		12h 15.1m	+47.10	Not in S.P.
	4231	Gal.	14.5p	—		12h 15.5m	+47.36	Not in S.P.
	4232	Gal.	14.6p	—		12h 15.5m	+47.35	Not in S.P.
	4233	Gal.	13.0p	1.0 x	0.4m	12h 14.6m	+07.54	
	4235	Gal.	12.6p	2.6 x	0.5m	12h 14.6m	+07.28	
	4236	Gal.	12.4v	20.0 x	5.0m	12h 14.3m	+69.45	
	4244	Gal.	11.9v	14.5 x	1.0m	12h 15.0m	+38.05	
	4246	Gal.	14.0p	—		12h 16.7m	+07.20	Not in S.P.
	4248	Gal.	13.9p	—		12h 16.6m	+47.33	Not in S.P.
	4254	Gal.	10.1v	4.6 x	3.9m	12h 16.3m	+14.42	
	4258	Gal.	8.6v	19.5 x	7.0m	12h 16.5m	+47.35	
	4260	Gal.	12.7p	2.0 x	0.9m	12h 16.8m	+06.23	
	4261	Gal.	10.3v	0.9 x	0.7m	12h 16.8m	+06.06	
	4264	Gal.	13.9p	—		12h 18.3m	+05.59	Not in S.P.
	4268	Gal.	13.9p	—		12h 18.5m	+05.26	Not in S.P.
	4270	Gal.	11.9v	1.2 x	0.4m	12h 17.3m	+05.44	
	4273	Gal.	11.6v	1.5 x	1.0m	12h 17.4m	+05.37	
	4281	Gal.	11.3v	1.1 x	0.6m	12h 17.8m	+05.40	
	4290	Gal.	12.7p	1.6 x	1.2m	12h 18.5m	+58.22	
	4300	Gal.	13.9p	—		12h 20.4m	+05.31	Not in S.P.
	4303	Gal.	10.1v	5.6 x	5.3m	12h 19.4m	+04.45	
	4312	Gal.	12.5p	—		12h 21.3m	+15.41	Not in S.P.
	4321	Gal.	10.6v	5.3 x	4.5m	12h 20.4m	+16.06	
	4346	Gal.	11.6v	1.9 x	0.7m	12h 21.0m	+47.16	
	4361	Pl.Nb.	10.8n/12.8st	81.0 s		12h 21.9m	−18.29	
	4374	Gal.	9.3v	1.6 x	1.4m	12h 22.6m	+13.10	
	4382	Gal.	9.3v	2.1 x	1.7m	12h 22.8m	+18.28	
	4388	Gal.	11.7p	5.0 x	0.9m	12h 23.3m	+12.56	
	4395	Gal.	10.7p	10.0 x	8.0m	12h 23.4m	+33.49	
	4406	Gal.	9.7v	2.1 x	1.4m	12h 23.7m	+13.13	
	4435	Gal.	10.3v	1.3 x	0.8m	12h 25.2m	+13.21	
	4438	Gal.	10.8v	8.0 x	3.0m	12h 25.3m	+13.17	
	4448	Gal.	11.4v	2.8 x	1.0m	12h 25.8m	+28.54	
	4472	Gal.	8.6v	2.8 x	1.8m	12h 27.3m	+08.16	
	4478	Gal.	10.9v	0.8 x	0.7m	12h 27.8m	+12.36	
	4485	Gal.	11.6v	1.5 x	0.8m	12h 28.2m	+41.58	
	4486	Gal.	9.2v	1.9 x	1.8m	12h 28.3m	+12.40	
	4490	Gal.	9.7v	5.6 x	2.1m	12h 28.3m	+41.55	
	4494	Gal.	9.6v	1.3 x	1.2m	12h 28.9m	+26.03	
	4501	Gal.	10.2v	5.5 x	2.4m	12h 29.5m	+14.42	
	4548	Gal.	10.8v	3.7 x	3.2m	12h 32.9m	+14.46	
	4552	Gal.	9.5v	1.3 x	1.3m	12h 33.1m	+12.50	
	4559	Gal.	10.6v	11.0 x	4.5m	12h 33.5m	+28.14	
	4562	Gal.	14.5p	—		12h 34.3m	+26.00	Not in S.P.
	4565	Gal.	10.2v	14.4 x	1.2m	12h 33.9m	+26.16	
	4569	Gal.	10.0v	7.5 x	2.2m	12h 34.3m	+13.26	

NAME		TYPE	MAGNITUDE	SIZE		R.A.	DEC.	COMMENTS
NGC	4576	Gal.	14.5p	—		12h 36.3m	+04.31	Not in S.P.
	4579	Gal.	9.2v	4.4 x	3.5m	12h 35.1m	+12.05	
	4590	Gb.	8.2v	2.9m		12h 36.8m	−26.29	
	4594	Gal.	8.7v	6.2 x	2.5m	12h 37.3m	−11.21	
	4618	Gal.	11.7v	3.5 x	3.0m	12h 39.2m	+41.25	
	4621	Gal.	9.6v	2.7 x	1.6m	12h 39.5m	+11.55	
	4625	Gal.	13.0p	—		12h 40.7m	+41.25	Not in S.P.
	4627	Gal.	13.5p	—		12h 40.8m	+32.43	Not in S.P.
	4631	Gal.	9.3v	12.6 x	1.5m	12h 39.8m	+32.49	
	4639	Gal.	12.1p	2.4 x	1.5m	12h 40.3m	+13.31	
	4647	Gal.	12.0p	2.0 x	1.5m	12h 41.0m	+11.51	
	4649	Gal.	8.9v	2.0 x	1.8m	12h 41.1m	+11.49	
	4654	Gal.	11.0p	4.2 x	2.2m	12h 41.4m	+13.23	
	4656	Gal.	11.2v	19.5 x	2.0m	12h 41.6m	+32.26	
	4736	Gal.	7.9v	5.0 x	3.5m	12h 48.6m	+41.23	
	4826	Gal.	8.8v	6.5 x	3.2m	12h 54.3m	+21.57	
	4868	Gal.	13.1p	1.1 x	1.0m	12h 56.8m	+37.35	
	4893	Gal.	15.5p	—		12h 58.9m	+37.19	Not in S.P.
	4914	Gal.	13.0p	1.0 x	0.8m	12h 58.4m	+37.35	
	4945	Gal.	9.2v	11.5 x	2.0m	13h 02.4m	−49.01	
	4976	Gal.	11.6p	2.0 x	1.5m	13h 05.9m	−49.14	
	5005	Gal.	9.8v	4.4 x	1.7m	13h 08.5m	+37.19	
	5014	Gal.	13.5p	—		13h 10.4m	+36.25	Not in S.P.
	5024	Gb.	7.6v	3.3m		13h 10.5m	+18.26	
	5033	Gal.	10.3v	9.9 x	4.8m	13h 11.2m	+36.51	
	5053	Gb.	10.5p	3.5m		13h 13.9m	+17.57	
	5107	Gal.	13.7p	—		13h 20.3m	+38.40	Not in S.P.
	5112	Gal.	12.6p	3.3 x	2.1m	13h 19.6m	+39.00	
	5128	Gal.	7.2p	10.0 x	8.0m	13h 22.4m	−42.45	
	5139	Gb.	3.7v	23.0m		13h 23.8m	−47.03	
	5194	Gal.	8.1v	10.0 x	5.5m	13h 27.8m	+47.27	
	5195	Gal.	8.4v	2.0 x	1.5m	13h 27.9m	+47.31	
	5198	Gal.	12.9p	0.6 x	0.5m	13h 28.2m	+46.56	
	5236	Gal.	8.0p	10.0 x	8.0m	13h 34.3m	−29.37	
	5253	Gal.	10.8p	4.0 x	1.5m	13h 37.1m	−31.24	
	5272	Gb.	6.4v	9.8m		13h 39.9m	+28.38	
	5286	Gb.	8.5p	1.6m		13h 43.0m	−51.07	
	5301	Gal.	13.0p	3.4 x	0.5m	13h 45.0m	+46.24	
	5377	Gal.	11.2v	3.0 x	0.6m	13h 54.3m	+47.27	
	5422	Gal.	11.5v	2.9 x	0.4m	13h 59.0m	+55.24	
	5448	Gal.	12.1p	4.0 x	1.2m	14h 00.9m	+49.25	
	5457	Gal.	9.6v	22.0 x	22.0m	14h 01.4m	+54.35	
	5473	Gal.	11.4v	1.2 x	0.6m	06h 42.8m	−27.35	
	5474	Gal.	11.4v	4.0 x	2.9m	14h 03.2m	+53.54	
	5480	Gal.	12.6p	1.1 x	0.9m	14h 04.6m	+50.57	
	5481	Gal.	13.5p	—		14h 05.7m	+50.51	Not in S.P.
	5533	Gal.	12.6p	1.8 x	0.8m	14h 14.1m	+35.35	
	5557	Gal.	11.6v	0.9 x	0.8m	14h 16.4m	+36.43	
	5566	Gal.	10.4v	5.6 x	1.1m	14h 17.8m	+04.11	
	5576	Gal.	11.7v	1.0 x	0.8m	14h 18.5m	+03.30	
	5614	Gal.	12.6p	1.0 x	0.8m	14h 22.0m	+35.05	
	5660	Gal.	12.3p	1.8 x	1.7m	14h 28.1m	+49.50	
	5676	Gal.	11.2v	3.0 x	1.3m	14h 31.0m	+49.41	
	5689	Gal.	11.4v	2.0 x	0.5m	14h 33.7m	+48.57	
	5693	Gal.	14.5p	—		14h 35.3m	+48.41	Not in S.P.

NAME		TYPE	MAGNITUDE	SIZE		R.A.	DEC.	COMMENTS
NGC	5694	Gb.	10.9p	2.2m		14h 36.7m	−26.19	
	5740	Gal.	11.7v	2.2 x	1.0m	14h 41.9m	+01.54	
	5746	Gal.	10.1v	6.2 x	0.8m	14h 42.3m	+02.10	
	5866	Gal.	10.8v	2.8 x	1.0m	15h 05.1m	+55.57	
	5882	Pl.Nb.	10.5n	7.0 s		15h 13.3m	−45.27	
	5885	Gal.	12.4p	2.4 x	2.4m	15h 12.4m	−09.53	
	5897	Gb.	10.9v	7.3m		15h 14.5m	−20.50	
	5904	Gb.	6.2v	12.7m		15h 16.0m	+02.16	
	5907	Gal.	11.3v	11.1 x	0.7m	15h 14.6m	+56.31	
	5982	Gal.	10.9v	1.2 x	0.8m	15h 37.6m	+59.32	
	5985	Gal.	11.4v	4.9 x	2.2m	15h 38.6m	+59.30	
	5986	Gb.	8.7v	3.7m		15h 42.8m	−37.37	
	6015	Gal.	11.7p	5.6 x	1.7m	15h 50.7m	+62.28	
	6052	Gal.	13.0p	0.8 x	0.6m	16h 03.1m	+20.41	
	6072	Pl.Nb.	14.1n/17.5st	50.0 x	30.0 s	16h 09.7m	−36.07	
	6093	Gb.	7.7v	3.3m		16h 14.1m	−22.52	
	6118	Gal.	12.3p	4.3 x	1.3m	16h 19.3m	−02.11	
	6121	Gb.	6.4v	14.0m		16h 20.6m	−26.24	
	6124	Cl.	6.3v	25.0m		16h 22.2m	−40.35	
	6139	Gb.	9.8p	1.3m		16h 24.3m	−38.44	
	6153	Pl.Nb.	11.5n	28.0 x	21.0 s	16h 28.0m	−40.08	
	6171	Gb.	9.2v	2.2m		16h 29.7m	−12.57	
	6181	Gal.	11.9v	2.0 x	0.9m	16h 30.1m	+19.56	
	6205	Gb.	5.7v	10.0m		16h 39.9m	+36.33	
	6207	Gal.	11.3v	2.0 x	1.1m	16h 41.3m	+36.56	
	6210	Pl.Nb.	9.7n/12.5st	20.0 x	13.0 s	16h 42.5m	+23.53	
	6218	Gb.	6.6v	9.3m		16h 44.6m	−01.52	
	6229	Gb.	8.7v	1.2m		16h 45.6m	+47.37	
	6239	Gal.	12.9p	2.1 x	0.8m	16h 48.4m	+42.50	
	6254	Gb.	6.7v	8.2m		16h 54.5m	−04.02	
	6266	Gb.	6.6v	4.3m		16h 58.1m	−30.03	
	6273	Gb.	6.6v	4.3m		16h 59.5m	−26.11	
	6284	Gb.	9.7v	1.5m		17h 01.5m	−24.41	
	6287	Gb.	9.9v	1.7m		17h 02.1m	−22.38	
	6293	Gb.	8.4v	1.9m		17h 07.1m	−26.30	
	6309	Pl.Nb.	11.6n/14.1st	19.0 x	10.0 s	17h 11.2m	−12.51	
	6333	Gb.	7.3v	2.4m		17h 16.2m	−18.28	
	6341	Gb.	6.1v	8.0m		17h 15.6m	+43.12	
	6342	Gb.	10.0v	0.5m		17h 18.2m	−19.32	
	6356	Gb.	8.7v	1.7m		17h 20.7m	−17.46	
	6369	Pl.Nb.	9.9n/16.6st	28.0 s		17h 26.3m	−23.44	
	6402	Gb.	7.7v	3.0m		17h 35.0m	−03.13	
	6405	Cl.	5.3v	25.0m		17h 36.8m	−32.11	About 50 st
	6440	Gb.	10.4v	0.7m		17h 45.9m	−20.21	
	6441	Gb.	8.4p	2.3m		17h 46.8m	−37.02	
	6444	Cl.	—	—		17h 48.6m	−34.52	Not in S.P.
	6445	Pl.Nb.	13.2n/19.1st	38.0 x	29.0 s	17h 46.3m	−20.00	
	6453	Gb.	11.2p	0.7m		17h 48.0m	−34.37	
	6475	Cl.	3.2v	60.0m		17h 50.7m	−34.48	About 50 st
	6494	Cl.	6.9v	25.0m		17h 54.0m	−19.01	About 120 st
	6496	Gb.	9.7p	2.2m		17h 55.5m	−44.15	
	6503	Gal.	9.6v	4.4 x	1.0m	17h 49.9m	+70.10	
	6514	B.N.	6.9st	29.0 x	27.0m	17h 58.9m	−23.02	
	6520	Op.Cl.	8.1v	5.0m		18h 00.3m	−27.54	About 25 st
	6523	B.N.	6.8st	60.0 x	35.0m	18h 01.6m	−24.20	
	6530	Cl.	6.3v	10.0m		18h 01.6m	−24.20	About 25 st

NAME		TYPE	MAGNITUDE	SIZE	R.A.	DEC.	COMMENTS
NGC	6531	Cl.	6.5v	10.0m	18h 01.8m	−22.30	About 50 st
	6541	Gb.	5.8p	6.3m	18h 04.4m	−43.44	
	6543	Pl.Nb.	8.8n/11.1st	22.0 s	17h 58.8m	+66.38	
	6563	Pl.Nb.	13.8n/18.3st	50.0 x 37.0 s	18h 08.8m	−33.53	
	6572	Pl.Nb.	9.6n/12.0st	16.0 x 13.0 s	18h 09.7m	+06.50	
	6574	Gal.	12.8p	0.9 x 0.7m	18h 09.5m	+14.58	
	6603	Cl.	4.6v	4.0m	18h 15.5m	−18.27	About 50 st
	6611	Cl.	6.4v	25.0m	18h 16.0m	−13.48	About 55 st
	6613	Cl.	7.5v	12.0m	18h 17.0m	−17.09	About 12 st
	6618	Cl.	7.5v	22.0m	18h 17.9m	−16.12	About 35 st
	6626	Gb.	7.3v	4.7m	18h 21.5m	−24.54	
	6629	Pl.Nb.	10.6n/13.6st	16.0 x 14.0 s	18h 22.7m	−23.14	
	6637	Gb.	8.9v	2.8m	18h 28.1m	−32.23	
	6643	Gal.	11.3v	3.0 x 1.3m	18h 21.2m	+74.33	
	6656	Gb.	5.9v	17.3m	18h 33.3m	−23.58	
	6681	Gb.	9.6v	2.5m	18h 40.0m	−32.21	
	6694	Cl.	9.3v	9.0m	18h 42.5m	−09.27	About 20 st
	6705	Cl.	6.3v	10.0m	18h 48.4m	−06.20	About 200 st
	6712	Gb.	8.9v	2.1m	18h 50.3m	−08.47	
	6715	Gb.	7.1v	2.1m	18h 52.0m	−30.32	
	6720	Pl.Nb.	9.3n/14.7st	83.0 x 59.0 s	18h 51.7m	+32.58	
	6723	Gb.	6.0p	5.8m	18h 56.2m	−36.42	
	6741	Pl.Nb.	11.7n/16.7st	9.0 x 7.0 s	19h 00.1m	−00.31	
	6751	Pl.Nb.	12.2n/13.3st	21.0 s	19h 03.2m	−06.05	
	6760	Gb.	10.7v	1.9m	19h 08.6m	+00.57	
	6779	Gb.	8.2v	1.8m	19h 14.6m	+30.05	
	6781	Pl.Nb.	12.5n/15.4st	106.0 s	19h 16.0m	+06.26	
	6804	Pl.Nb.	13.3n/13.3st	63.0 x 50.0 s	19h 29.2m	+09.07	
	6809	Gb.	4.4p	10.0m	19h 36.9m	−31.03	
	6818	Pl.Nb.	9.9n/15.0st	22.0 x 15.0 s	19h 41.1m	−14.17	
	6822	Gal.	9.2p	16.2 x 11.2m	19h 42.1m	−14.53	
	6826	Pl.Nb.	8.8n/10.8st	27.0 x 24.0 s	19h 43.4m	+50.24	
	6838	Gb.	—	6.1m	19h 51.5m	+18.39	
	6853	Pl.Nb.	7.6n/13.4st	480.0 x 240.0 s	19h 57.4m	+22.35	
	6864	Gb.	8.0v	1.9m	20h 03.2m	−22.04	
	6894	Pl.Nb.	14.4n/17.0st	44.0 s	20h 14.4m	+30.25	
	6913	Cl.	7.1v	12.0m	20h 22.2m	+38.21	About 20 st
	6946	Gal.	9.7p	9.0 x 7.5m	20h 33.9m	+59.58	
	6960	B.N.	—	70.0 x 6.0m	20h 43.6m	+30.32	
	6974	B.N.	—	—	20h 49.8m	+31.46	
	6981	Gb.	9.8v	2.0m	20h 50.7m	−12.44	
	6992	B.N.	—	78.0 x 8.0m	20h 54.3m	+31.30	
	6994	Cl.	9.0p	—	20h 56.4m	−12.50	Group/stars
	6995	Cl.	—	—	20h 56.0m	+31.07	Inv. in 6992
	7000	B.N.	1.3st	120.0 x 100.0m	20h 57.0m	+44.08	
	7008	Pl.Nb.	13.3n/12.9st	86.0 x 69.0 s	20h 59.1m	+54.21	
	7009	Pl.Nb.	8.4n/11.7st	44.0 x 26.0 s	21h 01.4m	−11.34	
	7078	Gb.	6.0v	7.4m	21h 27.6m	+11.57	
	7089	Gb.	6.3v	8.2m	21h 30.9m	−01.03	
	7092	Cl.	5.2v	30.0m	21h 30.4m	+48.13	About 25 st
	7099	Gb.	8.4v	5.7m	21h 37.5m	−23.25	
	7177	Gal.	12.0p	2.1 x 1.1m	21h 58.3m	+17.29	
	7184	Gal.	12.0p	5.1 x 0.9m	21h 59.9m	−21.04	
	7217	Gal.	11.0p	2.6 x 2.3m	22h 05.6m	+31.07	
	7293	Pl.Nb.	6.5n/13.3st	900.0 x 720.0 s	22h 27.0m	−21.06	

NAME	TYPE	MAGNITUDE	SIZE	R.A.	DEC.	COMMENTS
NGC 7331	Gal.	9.7v	10.0 x 2.3m	22h 34.8m	+34.10	
7332	Gal.	11.8p	2.3 x 0.6m	22h 35.0m	+23.32	
7448	Gal.	11.2v	2.0 x 1.0m	22h 57.6m	+15.43	
7457	Gal.	12.2v	1.9 x 1.0m	22h 58.6m	+29.53	
7479	Gal.	11.6v	3.4 x 2.6m	23h 02.4m	+12.03	
7510	Cl.	8.8v	2.0m	23h 09.2m	+60.18	About 27 st
7606	Gal.	11.5v	4.4 x 1.5m	23h 16.5m	−08.46	
7635	Pl.Nb.	8.5n/8.5st	205.0 x 180.0 s	23h 18.5m	+60.54	
7640	Gal.	11.3p	11.0 x 1.4m	23h 19.7m	+40.35	
7654	Cl.	7.3v	12.0m	23h 22.0m	+61.20	About 120 st
7662	Pl.Nb.	8.9n/12.5st	32.0 x 28.0 s	23h 23.5m	+42.14	
7678	Gal.	12.5p	1.7 x 1.1m	23h 26.1m	+22.09	
7723	Gal.	11.1v	2.2 x 1.6m	23h 36.4m	−13.14	
7727	Gal.	10.7v	2.7m	23h 37.3m	−12.34	
7741	Gal.	11.6p	3.0 x 2.0m	23h 41.4m	+25.48	
IC 289	Pl.Nb.	12.3n/15.0st	45.0 x 30.0 s	03h 06.2m	+61.08	
342	Gal.	12.0p	15.0 x 15.0m	03h 41.9m	+67.57	
349	B.N.	—	30.0 x 30.0m	03h 43.2m	+23.36	
351	Pl.Nb.	12.4n/15.0st	8.0 x 6.0 s	03h 44.3m	+34.54	
361	Cl.	11.2v	6.0m	04h 14.8m	+58.11	About 40 st
410	B.N.	—	23.0 x 20.0m	05h 19.3m	+33.28	
418	Pl.Nb.	12.0n/10.9st	14.0 x 11.0 s	05h 25.4m	−12.44	
434	B.N.	—	60.0 x 10.0m	05h 38.6m	−2.26	
724	Gal.	13.8p	—	11h 41.0m	+09.13	Not in S.P.
1287	B.N.	5.8st	44.0 x 34.0m	18h 27.6m	−10.50	
1295	Pl.Nb.	15.0n	120.0 x 90.0 s	18h 51.9m	−08.51	
1470	Pl.Nb.	8.1n/11.9st	70.0 x 45.0 s	23h 03.2m	+59.59	
1727	Gal.	12.2p	—	01h 44.6m	+27.05	
1747	Pl.Nb.	13.6n/15.0st	13.0 s	01h 53.8m	+63.04	
2003	Pl.Nb.	12.6n/18.4st	5.0 s	03h 53.2m	+33.44	
2149	Pl.Nb.	9.9n/14.0st	15.0 x 10.0 s	05h 52.6m	+46.07	
2165	Pl.Nb.	12.5n/16.8st	9.0 x 7.0 s	06h 19.6m	−12.57	
2395	Cl.	4.6v	10.0m	08h 43.4m	−48.00	About 16 st
2627	Gal.	12.8p	2.0 x 1.6m	11h 07.5m	−23.28	
3568	Pl.Nb.	11.6n/12.0st	18.0 s	11h 32.4m	+82.51	
4406	Pl.Nb.	10.6n	100.0 x 37.0 s	14h 19.3m	−43.55	
4593	Pl.Nb.	10.2n/10.2st	15.0 x 11.0 s	16h 09.5m	+12.12	
4634	Pl.Nb.	12.3n/17.4st	20.0 x 9.0 s	16h 58.5m	−21.44	
4725	Cl.	6.5v	40.4m	18h 28.8m	−19.17	About 50 st
5146	B.N.	10.0st	12.0 x 12.0 s	21h 51.3m	+47.02	
B 33	D.N.	—	—	—	—	Horsehead Nb.
72	D.N.	—	30.0m	17h 21.0m	−23.35	"S" Neb.
86	D.N.	—	4.5 x 3.0m	18h 00.0m	−27.50	
92	D.N.	—	15.0m	18h 12.7m	−18.20	
142	D.N.	—	40.0m	19h 37.0m	+10.30	
143	D.N.	—	30.0m	19h 38.0m	+11.00	
Mel 22	Cl.	1.4v	100.0m	03h 43.9m	+23.58	About 130 st
Winnecke 4	D.S.	9.0/9.3	—	12h 20.0m	+58.22	2 st (M40)
New 1	Gal.	12.8p	3.5 x 3.5m	01h 02.6m	−06.29	

NOTE:

All co-ordinates are for 1950 except for those objects marked "Not in S.P.;" many of which are 1975 co-ordinates.

NEW GENERAL CATALOG (NGC)

NGC	DESCRIPTION
40	Pl.Nb. 10.2 neb/11.4 star; 8 in. RFL F/5 w/16mmKo, 10.2mmO. Small, diffuse with a very bright compact center. Round with a slight blue color, fuzzy outer envelope. Reminds me of a compact galaxy with a bright core. With the 10.2mm ocular a faint star was seen just below the nebula.
45	Gal. 12.1p; 8 in. RFL F/5 w/16mmKo. Very dim, averted vision helps. Large and roundish, no definite edges seen, even brightness throughout, touching a bright star, fainter than NGC 281.
55	Gal. 7.8p; 8 in. Celestron w/25mmK. Very large and bright object, bright core, very much extended. Reminds me of NGC 253. Impressive.
185	Gal. 11.0p; 6 in. RFL F/8 w/25mmO. Round, medium sized, averted vision helps with the envelope, no bright core seen.
205	Gal. 9.4p; 8 in. RFL F/5 w/25mmO. Bright patch appearance, large and elliptical, even brightness throughout. Also seen with a 6 in. telescope.
206	Bright patch involved in M31; 10 in. RFL F/5.6, 16mmK0. This bright patch was very obvious, in fact it was brighter than the surrounding arm of M31, in which NGC 206 is located. It can be found near the edge of the south-western arm.
221 (M32)	Gal. 8.7v; 8 in. RFL F/5 w/25mmO. Medium sized with a very bright core, thin fuzzy envelope, round shape. All three galaxies (M31, M32 & NGC 205) fit into the same field of view.
224 (M31)	Gal. 4.8v; 8 in. RFL F/5 w/32mmP. Extremely bright and large with averted vision it extends almost two fields of view. Central core is bright and large. The envelope surrounding the nucleus is considerably bright. Normally one dark lane can be seen, usually be-

NGC 224 (M31) Andromeda Galaxy, NGC 221 (M32) bottom right, NGC 205 left of M31

NGC 253 top right, NGC 288 bottom left

NGC	DESCRIPTION
	ing 3/4 of the field of view long. Under favorable conditions a second dark lane, about 1/6 of the field long, can be seen. Sometimes the "straight edge" of M31 between the nucleus of M31 and NGC 205 can be seen. Impressive. See NGC 206. M31 can be seen with the naked eye.
246	Pl.Nb. 8.5 neb/11.5 star; 8 in. RFL F/5 w/16mmKo. Large, easily seen as a round diffuse glow behind three stars of similar brightness, easy. A fainter fourth star was glimpsed on the edge of the diffuse glow. No central star was seen. A 6 in. telescope shows NGC 246 as three stars appearing in luminosity.
247	Gal. 10.7p; 8 in. RFL F/5 w/16mmKo. Very large, fills almost 1/2 field of view. Elongated with the southern tip shorter but more definite than the northern tip. Star seen on edge of southern tip. Core has patch appearance and appears off center. Impressive. Also seen in a 6 in. telescope.
253	Gal. 8.9v; 6 in. RFL F/8 w/25mmO. Very large about 1/3 field of view long, very bright core, mottling suspected on envelope's western edge. Very impressive. With an 8 in. Celestron, four or five foreground stars were seen in the nebula.
255	Gal. 12.4p; 8 in. RFL F/5 w/16mmKo. Small faint patch of light, elliptical shaped. Seen in same field as NGC 246.
281	B.N.; 8 in. RFL F/5 w/25mmO. Easily seen as a large, diffuse, roundish object, with a bright 8.6 mag. star seen off center. This nebula reminds me of NGC 2174-5 in Orion. Under favorable conditions this nebula (281) can be seen through a 10 x 40 finderscope as a fuzzy patch of light.
288	Gb.Cl. 7.2p; 8 in. Celestron w/25mmK. Large, bright, round with individual stars at seen the edges. NGC 288 is larger than M15 but otherwise they appear similar.
300	Gal. 11.3p; 6 in. RFL F/8 w/25mmO. Appears nearly face-on, even brightness throughout, faint. Averted vision helps.
404	Gal. 10.7v; 8 in. RFL F/5 w/16mmKo. Easily seen as a medium sized, round patch of light. Even brightness throughout. NGC 404 is omitted from most amateur atlases because it is close to the bright star Beta Andromeda. It can be found on the northwest edge of the star. Try placing the star just outside the field or block the light from the outside with a bar or other implement.
428	Gal. 11.7p; 8 in. RFL F/5 w/16mmKo. Easily seen as a round object having the patch appearance with no sharp edges. Even brightness throughout. Two stars of similar brightness seen just below this object.
488	Gal. 11.1v; 6 in. RFL F/8 w/25mmO. Easily seen as a round object with a bright core surrounded by an envelope. Averted vision helps on the envelope. This galaxy looks similar to NGC 524 except that 488 looks a little larger with a slightly fainter envelope.

NGC 598 (M33)

NGC	DESCRIPTION
524	Gal. 11.1v; 6 in. RFL F/8 w/25mmO. Easily seen as a round object, a bright core surrounded by a fainter envelope.
581 (M103)	Cl. 7.4v; 8 in. RFL F/5 w/16mmKo. Bright compact arrowhead shaped cluster. About 25 or so total stars with six bright stars. The brightest star is at the tip of the arrowhead and has a slight orange color. This cluster is more compact than NGC 654. No background glow seen. This cluster was also seen with a 2.4 in. refractor (20mm ocular) where it appeared as a few stars in an arrowhead shape, embedded in a luminous glow.
598 (M33)	Gal. 6.7v; 8 in. RFL F/5 w/25mmO. Very large, bright, seen face on. Not an even brightness throughout. Instead averted vision shows some hint of spiral structure radiating out from the brighter core area. Can be seen through a 5 x 30 finder as a large dim patch of light. Impressive under clear, dark skies.
604	Bt.Kt.; 8 in. Celestron F/10 w/28mmO. Small but very obvious bright knot seen in northeast portion of the field just beyond the outer envelope of M33. This knot was slightly elliptical, small, fuzzy but very obvious.
628 (M74)	Gal. 10.2v mag; 6 in. RFL F/8 w/25mmO. Faint, roundish, fairly good sized object, slightly brighter core, reminds me a little of M33 but 628 is much smaller, averted vision helps.
650-1 (M76)	Pl.Nb. 12.2 neb/16.6 star; 10 in. RFL F/5 w/25mmO. Obvious patch of light, twice as long as it is wide. Has a definite "bow-tie" shape with a much less luminous center, almost separating each half. Southern nodule is slightly brighter than the northern. This difference was confirmed with a 6mm ocular.
654	Cl. 9.1v; 8 in. RFL F/5 w/16mmKo. Sparse, small and not too impressive, irregular shape somewhat like that of an opened umbrella. A bright red star is involved. This cluster was seen with a 3-1/2 in. Questar telescope.
659	Cl. 9.8v; 8 in. RFL F/5 w/16mmKo. Small, very sparse, about ten stars, irregular shape, could easily be missed. With a 3-1/2 in. Questar the cluster was almost non-existant.
663	Cl. 7.1v; 8 in. RFL F/5 w/16mmKo. Larger than M103, NGC 654 or NGC 659. Irregular shape, not too compact, about 30-40 stars, no background nebulosity. A "darker area" was noticed, shaped almost like a squared off letter "S." Two faint extensions go out from 663 towards the cluster 659. When 663 was placed at one edge of the field of view, NGC 659 was at the opposite end. When 663 was placed at the opposite end of the field, then NGC 654 was seen in the same field. NGC 663 was seen with a 3-1/2 in. Questar.
670	Gal. 13.0p; 10 in. RFL F/5.6 w/16mmKo. Just north of NGC 672, about 1/2 degree. Very small, round, compact galaxy, fuzzy object, hard to spot.

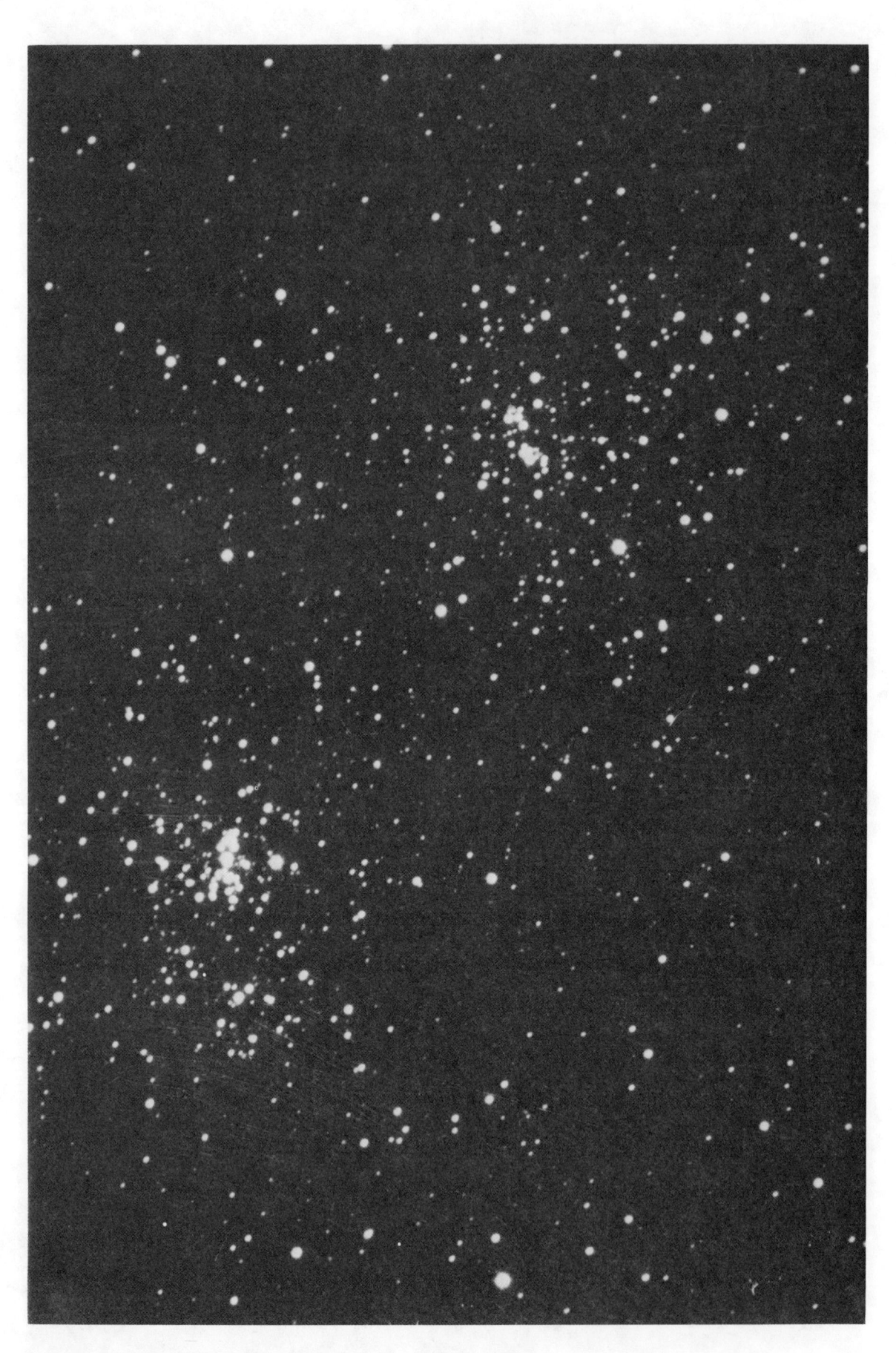

Double Cluster in Perseus NGC 869 left & NGC 884 right

NGC	DESCRIPTION
672	Gal. 12.2p; 10 in. RFL F/5.6 w/16mmKo. Fairly large, elongated, even brightness throughout. A star seen on eastern tip and a less bright star seen on western tip. Easy. Close to IC1727.
736	Gal. 13.6p; 10 in. RFL F/5.6 w/16mmKo. Elongated shape with a faint star on northern edge, even brightness throughout. Not found in Skalnate Pleso.
750-1	Gal. 12.9p; 10 in. RFL F/5.6 w/16mmKo. Elongated with one side (750) brighter than the other (751). Together they are smaller and fainter than NGC 925. Both parts appear similar in size.
752	Cl. 7.0v; 6 in. RFL F/8 w/25mmO. Large open cluster of loose stars. A few brighter stars stand out. Larger than one field of view. This object can be seen with the naked eye and is easier to see than M33 but fainter than M31.
772	Gal. 10.9v; 6 in. RFL F/8 w/25mmO. Very faint, may be elliptical, averted vision shows a slightly brighter core.
777	Gal. 13.0p; 10 in. RFL F/5.6 w/16mmKo. About 1/2 degree south of NGC 783. Roundish with a bright compact nucleus. It appeared brighter than both NGC 783 or NGC 750-1.
783 (IC1765)	Gal. 12.8p; 10 in. RFL F/5.6 w/16mmKo. Even brightness throughout. Patch appearance with no definite shape. Star seen on western and eastern sides. Not in Skalnate Pleso.
784	Gal. 12.1p; 10 in. RFL F/5.6 w/16mmKo. Fairly large, elongated north—south direction, averted vision shows a very faint core, has a general patch appearance surrounded by faint stars. Hard.
812	Gal. 12.8p; 8 in. RFL F/5 w/16mmKo. Small, very faint, averted vision needed to see it, shape may be edge on with a thick core. Using a 25mm ocular, NGC 812 was not seen. Not in Skalnate Pleso Atlas.
846	Gal. 13.2p; 8 in. RFL F/5 w/16mmKo. Faint and round but averted vision is not needed once spotted. Brighter and slightly larger than NGC 812. Not in Skalnate Pleso.
869	Cl. 4.4v; 10 in. RFL F/5.6 w/25mmO. The core area is a very compact arrowhead shaped object made up of faint stars. The cluster itself consists of "small" stars radiating in all directions from the center. Two bright yellow stars are seen near the center.
884	Cl. 4.7v; 10 in. RFL F/5.6 w/25mmO. Irregular shaped cluster with no compact center, fewer bright stars than NGC 869. A bright star with a yellow tint is seen off center in the cluster.
890	Gal. 12.7p; 10 in. RFL F/5.6 w/16mmKo. Much smaller than NGC 925. Small with a bright nucleus, small round envelope.
891	Gal. 10.9p; 10 in. RFL F/5.6 w/16mmKo. Very long edge on, thick core, slight brightening towards center. Dark lane suspected with

NGC	DESCRIPTION
	averted vision. Bright star seen just south of nucleus, star seen on northern edge, non-uniform brightness throughout galaxy envelope. Impressive.
925	Gal. 10.5p; 10 in. RFL F/5.6 w/16mmKo. Easily seen as an irregular patch of light. Large with an extensive envelope, no bright core but a gradually brightening middle seen with averted vision. Some foreground stars seen.
936	Gal. 10.7 mag; 8 in. Celestron F/10 w/16mmKo. Small with an obvious outer envelope, much brighter almost stellar cone. Very easy to see.
941	Gal. 12.8p; 8 in. Celestron F/10 w/16mmKo. Seen with averted vision as an extremely faint patch, no definite shape, hard to see.
949	Gal. 12.7v; 10 in. RFL F/5.6 w/16mmKo. Fairly bright, elongated, patch appearance. Easier to see than 890 but harder than 925.
1023	Gal. 10.5p; 10 in. RFL F/5.6 w/25mmO. Obvious as a bright, compact, round core with two long faint extensions. Easy. Also seen with a 6 in. telescope.
1032	Gal. 13.2p; 8 in. RFL F/5 w/16mmKo. Small, use averted vision to locate. Has a patch appearance with a somewhat elliptical shape, even brightness throughout.
1035	Gal. 12.8p; 6 in. RFL F/8 w/25mmO. Thin, very much extended, faint, averted vision helps to locate.
1039 (M34)	Cl. 5.5v; 10 in. RFL F/5.6 w/25mmO. Very large cluster, filling the field of view. Approximately; a dozen or so stars with no specific pattern. Two long curving arms, composed of very faint stars, were seen to radiate out from the center of the cluster, in opposite directions. Using averted vision a third shorter, fainter arm was seen.
1048	Gal. 12.5p; 6 in. RFL F/8 w/25mmO. Very diffuse, round, face-on galaxy. Even brightness throughout. Use averted vision to locate.
1052	Gal. 11.2v; 6 in. RFL F/8 w/25mmO. Round with a much brighter core, small fuzzy envelope. Brighter than 1048 or 1045.
1055	Gal. 11.4p; 8 in. RFL F/5 w/16mmKo. Elliptical with a bright core, patch appearance, easy. Seen in same field as M77.
1058	Gal. 11.7p; 6 in. RFL F/8 w/25mmO. Larger than N1023, round, patch appearance, faint, use averted vision. Hard.
1068 (M77)	Gal. 8.9v; 8 in. RFL F/5 w/16mmKo. Bright, large, with a bright condensed nucleus, easy. Seen with a 6 in. telescope. Under clear, dark skies, a sweep around M77 (immediate area) will show many faint galaxies in the 13th—14th magnitude range. A scope of 8 in. or larger is recommended for this project.

NGC	DESCRIPTION
1073	Gal. 11.4p; 8 in. RFL F/5 w/16mmKo. Faint, round with possible brightening towards the center, has patch appearance.
1087	Gal. 11.9v; 8 in. RFL F/5 w/16mmKo. Brighter than 1090. Round, even brightness throughout, easy. In same field as 1090, both are about the same size. Seen with a 6 in. telescope.
1090	Gal. 12.5p; 8 in. RFL F/5 w/16mmKo. Very much extended, slight brightening towards the center, easy.
1094	Gal. 13.5p; 8 in. RFL F/5 w/16mmKo. Seen with averted vision as a small roundish patch of light. Slightly fainter than NGC 45. Not far from NGC 1087, 1090, just outside field.
1097	Gal. 10.6p; 6 in. RFL F/8 w/25mmO. Very much extended with a bright core, easy.
1232	Gal. 10.5p; 6 in. RFL F/8 w/25mmO. Large, face on with a slightly brighter core, easy.
1316	Gal. 10.1p; 8 in. RFL F/5 w/25mmO. Small, round with a bright core, easy. In same field as 1317.
1317	Gal. 12.2p; 8 in. RFL F/5 w/25mmO. Fainter and smaller than 1316. Round with a slightly brighter core which appears starlike with averted vision. Because 1316 is so bright compared to 1317 and because both galaxies are in the same field, it makes locating 1317 more difficult than it would otherwise be.
1332	Gal. 10.4v; 6 in. RFL F/8 w/25mmO. Extended object with a bright core, small, easy.
1365	Gal. 11.2p; 8 in. RFL F/5 w/25mmO. Largest of nine galaxies nearly in the same field, including; NGC 1374, 1379, 1381, 1386, 1387, 1389, 1399, 1404 and 1365. NGC 1365 appeared bright, round, has a steady increase in brightness towards the center, very easy.
1374	Gal. 12.4p; 8 in. RFL F/5 w/25mmO. Slightly fainter than 1381, round, use averted vision to locate.
1379	Gal. 12.3p; 8 in. RFL F/5 w/25mmO. Slightly brighter than 1381 but slightly fainter than 1387, round, even brightness throughout.
1380	Gal. 11.4p; 8 in. RFL F/5 w/25mmO. Elliptical with a brighter fuzzy core, core larger than most, fainter than 1399, easy.
1381	Gal. 12.6p; 8 in. RFL F/5 w/25mmO. Smaller and fainter than 1399, round with a brighter core, easy.
1386	Gal. 12.4p; 8 in. RFL F/5 w/15mmO. Faint and small, extended, possible brighter core with averted vision. Hard.
1387	Gal. 12.1p; 8 in. RFL F/5 w/25mmO. Very faint and small, must use averted vision to locate. Hard.

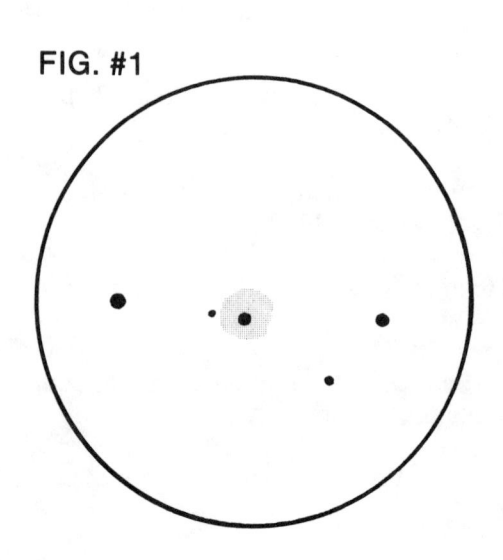

NGC	DESCRIPTION
1389	Gal. 12.8p; 8 in. RFL F/5 w/25mmO. Faint, smaller than 1386, patch appearance, shape. Hardest of group to see.
1399	Gal. 10.9p; 8 in. RFL F/5 w/25mmO. Round, brighter with a larger envelope than 1386, very easy.
1404	Gal. 11.5p; 8 in. RFL F/5 w/25mmO. Brightness similar to 1386, round, brighter core than 1386, appears as a double nebula. With a 10mm ocular the "double" part of the nebula turns out to be a faint star, almost touching the edge of the envelope.
1427	Gal. 12.4p; 8 in. RFL F/5 w/25mmO. May be elongated, with a slightly brighter core, averted vision helps.
1437	Gal. 12.9p; 8 in. RFL F/5 w/25mmO. Round, even brightness throughout, use averted vision to locate.
1491	Bt.Nb.; 8 in. Celestron F/10 w/40mmO, 16mmKo (40mm). Round nebulous glow surrounding an obvious star, off center. The nebulous shell is definitely brighter on the western side of the star. The star itself is off center near the eastern portion of the nebula. The outer shell did not appear perfectly round and this nebula could be found while sweeping the area. (16mm)—Much harder to see the nebulosity.
1501	Pl.Nb. 13.3 neb/13.4 star; 8 in. RFL F/5 w/16mmKo. Easily seen as a dim disk, small, uneven brightness with a possible dark center. Seen through a 3-1/2 in. Questar.
1502	Cl. 5.3v; 8 in. RFL F/5 w/16mmKo. Arrowhead shaped, resolvable, no background glow, Struve 485 is a prominent double star (white). Reminds me of M103.
1514	Pl.Nb. 10.8 neb/9.7 star; 10 in. RFL F/5.6 w/25mmO. Very bright central star with a round outer envelope. Blinking effect prominent with 25mm ocular but not with 16mm ocular. Seen with a 6 in. telescope.

FIG. #1

NGC 1514

10 in. F/5.5 with 16mm ocular

Outer shell not as prominent as with NGC 1931. Star to left of planetary is brightest, star on right extreme is second, central star in planetary is third, star on right bottom is fourth while star nearest to planetary on left edge is the faintest.

NGC	DESCRIPTION
1535	Pl.Nb. 9.3 neb/11.8 star; 6 in. RFL F/8 w/18mmO. Very bright, bluish-green color, disk prominent, even brightness throughout. Reminds me of NGC 7662.
1579	B.N.; 10 in. RFL F/5.6 w/25mmO. Very diffuse patch of light, with a brighter circular area on the northern edge. The nebula is a medium sized object similar to the Merope nebula in the Pleiades, except a little more "Tear Drop" shaped. The brighter area is at the tip of the tear drop.
1625	Gal. 13.1p; 10 in. RFL F/5.5 w/16mmG. Easy, edge on galaxy, small, elongated east—west. 10.2mm—Faint star on eastern tip. 25mmKo—Seen as a very small nebulous patch, use averted vision.
1637	Gal. 12.1v; 6 in. RFL F/8 w/25mmO. Faint, round smudge. A brighter core seen with averted vision. Medium sized overall.
1638	Gal. 13.1p; 10 in. RFL F/5.5 w/16mmG. Small but obvious, round face-on, definite starlike nucleus. Smaller and fainter than NGC 1637 but slightly larger and brighter than NGC 1625. Seen with 24mm as a small patch of light.
1647	Cl. 6.3v; 6 in. RFL F/8 w/25mmO. Loose open cluster, pentagon shape almost fills eyepiece, most all stars appear to be the same brightness.
1720	Gal. 13.0p; 8 in. RFL F/5 w/16mmKo. Long, thin, larger than 1726 but fainter. Even brightness throughout, use averted vision at first, then not needed. Not in Skalnate Pleso. Seen in 6 in.
1726	Gal. 13.0p; 8 in. RFL F/5 w/16mmKo. Round, easily seen being brighter and smaller than 1720. A stellar nucleus is suspected. In same field as 1720. Seen in a 6 in. RFL.
1746	Cl. 6.0v; 6 in. RFL F/8 w/25mmO. Fills eyepiece with loose stars, bright stars scattered throughout. No definite shape or center.
1784	Gal. 12.4p; 10 in. RFL F/5.5 w/16mmG. Situated among four stars of similar brightness. The galaxy looks elliptical with one faint star on north tip just above center of galaxy. Two other stars are seen, one on each tip of the two arms or extensions. Medium sized patch of light with no definite core but a gradual brightening towards the center is apparent. Easy.
1792	Gal. 10.7p; 6 in. RFL F/8 w/25mmO. Elliptical shape, bright with a slightly brighter core, easy. In same field as 1808.
1807	Cl. 7.8v; 2.4 in. RR F/12 w/20mmHy. No particular shape, about 15—20 stars, same brightness as 1817 but more compact.
1808	Gal. 11.2p; 6 in. RFL F/8 w/25mmO. Elliptical shape, even brightness throughout, easy. Fainter and smaller than 1792.

NGC 1907

NGC 1912 (M38)

NGC	DESCRIPTION
1817	Cl. 7.9v; 2.4 in. RR F/12 w/20mmHy. Shaped somewhat like the letter "X." About 10—15 stars, less compact than 1807.
1851	Gb.Cl. 8.1v; 6 in. RFL F/8 w/25mmO. Round, small with a very bright nucleus, fuzzy outer shell, no individual stars seen.
1893	Cl. 8.0v; 10 in. RFL F/5 w/16mmKo. Cluster is 1/4 size of the field of view. Large, shaped similar to an inverted "Y" with the two shorter extensions widely separated. About six brighter stars forming the main "Y" shape, with minor stars filling out this "Y." Associated with Bright Neb. IC410.
1904 (M79)	Gb.Cl. 8.4v; 8 in. RFL F/5 w/16mmKo. Bright, round, resolved except for core area. Smaller than M15. Also seen through 4-1/4 in. RFL and 6 in. RFL.
1907	Cl. 9.9v; 10 in. RFL F/5 w/16mmKo. Very small but obvious, about 20 stars around a compact center. M38 and 1907 are in the same field.
1912 (M38)	Cl. 7.4v; 10 in. RFL F/5 w/16mmKo. About the same size as M37 but more scattered (stars) and containing fewer stars. More compact than M36 and M38 has more stars. The stars in M38 are of uniform brightness.
1931	B.N.; 10 in. RFL F/5 w/16mmKo, 6.8mmO. Very obvious small patch of light, oval with two or three stars close together, inside this fuzzy patch. 6.8mm—Three stars inside, medium sized object. The two stars closest together are of similar magnitude and are the brightest of the group. The third star is somewhat fainter. Two fainter stars are seen, one on each end of the brighter three main stars. A total of five stars are seen inside this nebula.

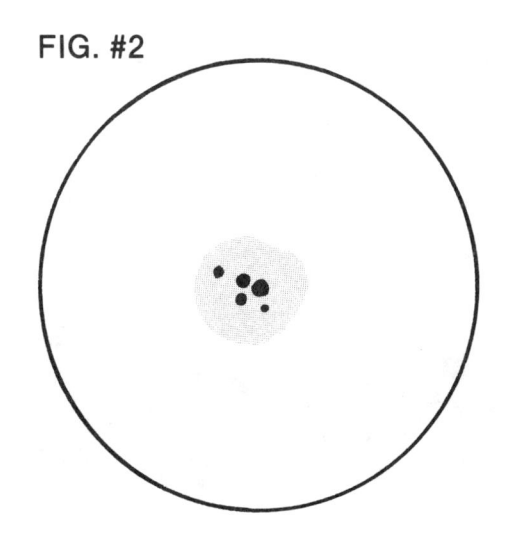

FIG. #2

NGC 1931

10 in. F/5.5 with 6.8mm ocular

Five stars total seen within the shell. The two "eyes" are of equal magnitude and are the brightest stars. The "nose" star is second, star to left of "eyes" is third, while the star just right of and below "eyes" is the faintest.

Crab Nebula NGC 1952 (M1)

NGC 1960 (M36)

NGC	DESCRIPTION
1952 (M1)	Pl.Nb. 8.4 neb/15.9 star; 8 in. RFL F/5 w/16mmKo. Large and bright with irregular edges, dark protrusion on top left. Very impressive. Easily seen with a 6 in. RFL.
1960 (M36)	Cl. 6.3v; 10 in. RFL F/5 w/16mmKo. About the same size as M37 but containing less stars and being more loose. Bright with a slightly compact center. Contains a few more brighter stars than does M37. Seen in finderscope. Easy.
1964	Gal. 11.6p; 6 in. RFL F/8 w/25mmO. Use averted vision to locate, elliptical shape with a stellar center. Close to two brighter stars (9-10 mag).
1976 (M42)	B.N.; 8 in. RFL F/5 w/16mmKo. Shaped like a cowboy hat, extremely bright. Where the brim extends on both sides, they were seen to continue until they met, forming an arc over the hat itself, This arc can be seen only during better than average seeing conditions. The intrusion of dark gas is obvious near the bright center of the "hat." The four stars in the trapezium are obvious. Using a 16 in. Cass. in Tucson, the beauty of the nebulous wisps were lost and only the brighter core area remained. Looked similar to Herschels drawing. This nebula shows different views to the observer at different times. The sky conditions are an important factor. Clear, dark, moonless nights with steady air are the best. Can be seen with the naked eye as a small patch of light.
1982 (M43)	B.N.; 6 in. RFL F/8 w/25mmO. Smaller and less bright than its neighbor (M42) to the south, but still an impressive sight. Centered on a bright (9 mag.) star. Nebula is mostly round with one extended flat side. If this nebula were in some other part of the sky, it would appear more impressive, not being overshadowed by the brighter, larger M42.
1999	B.N. 9.5 star; 8 in. RFL F/5 w/25mmO. Located just south of M42. It appears as a blue-white star out of focus, bright.
2022	Pl.Nb. 12.8 neb/14.6 star; 8 in. RFL F/5 w/16mmKo. Pale green disk, small, easily seen, field has only a few stars in it. Seen with a 6 in. scope.
2023	Bt.Nb.; 10 in. RFL F/5.5 w/16mmKo. Very obvious, medium sized, round bright nebula with a very bright condensed center, easy.
2024	B.N. 1.9 star; 6 in. RFL F/8 w/25mmO. Large, round, a very obvious thick dark band cuts the nebula in half. Another dark band, thinner and shorter, extends from the southeast portion of the larger dark band and travels northeast through the bright nebula. Easy.
2068 (M78)	B.N. 10.3 star; 8 in. RFL F/5 w/16mmKo. Very bright fuzzy core with a very bright roundish outer envelope. Gray color. Core is off center in envelope and envelope is very diffuse. Not a large object. Seen through 6 in.
	10 in. F/5.5 with 16mm ocular. A somewhat oval shaped object, narrower at the preceding edge, sharp edge, green color, two

Orion Nebula NGC 1976 (M42) & NGC 1982 (M43)

NGC 2099

NGC	DESCRIPTION
	bright stars in northern part near edge, one fainter star on opposite southern edge. The brightest portion of the nebula is the area around the two brighter stars, in the northern section. From here, the nebulosity fans out in all directions except to the north and fades towards the south, just past the faint star mentioned. The north edge of this object is more sharply defined than the rest. Just north of the main nebula, a "bright" star is incased in nebulosity, easy to see. See Fig. #3. The main nebulosity was seen in a 6 x 40 finderscope and in a pair of 7 x 35 binoculars... knowing where to look. It appeared through both of these instruments as a small green disk.

FIG. #3

NGC 2068

10 in. F/5.5 with 16mm ocular

The brightest part of the nebulosity is that immediately around the two bright "eyes."

2090	Gal. 12.4p; 8 in. RFL F/5 w/25mmO. Small, round fuzzy core, extended envelope. Envelope is small and averted vision will help. The core area is easily seen.
2099 (M37)	Cl. 6.2v; 10 in. F/5 w/16mmKo. Of the three Messier objects in Auriga (M36, M37, M38), this one is the most impressive. It is the largest of the trio and seems to contain the most stars. The stars are generally fainter than the stars in M36 or M38 but this cluster is more compact. A very obvious dark area shaped somewhat like a "T" can be seen. The base of this "T" is located near the center of the cluster. This dark area covers about 1/5 of the area of the cluster. Overall shape of the cluster, due to this dark area, is like that of a blacksmith's anvil. The main portion of this cluster fills about 1/4 of the field but due to the high number of background stars, the cluster seems to fill the entire field. The cluster contains one bright red star, near the center of the cluster, just below the base of the "T."
2126	Cl. 9.8; 10 in. RFL F/5 w/16mmKo. Very small and slightly compact cluster, 10th mag. stars in an irregular shape. Very bright star on northeast edge.
2139	Gal. 11.9p; 6 in. RFL F/8 w/25mmO. Small, round with a slightly brighter fuzzy core. Slightly larger and dimmer than 2196.

NGC 2168 (M35) Cluster top right, NGC 2158 to right of M35, NGC 2174-5 bottom

NGC	DESCRIPTION
2146	Gal. 11.3p; 8 in. RFL F/5 w/25mmO. Bright fuzzy core off center. Envelope is extended and is easy to see.
2158	Cl. 12.5v; 6 in. RFL F/8 w/25mmO. Seen as a small mottled cluster at the tip of M35. Easily distinguished from the background stars.
2168 (M35)	Cl. 5.3v; 6 in. RFL F/8 w/25mmO. This cluster appears like a cone with the tip missing. The stars are about equal brightness and a dark background gives it a "jewel" appearance. It almost fills the eyepiece. Impressive.
2169	Cl. 6.4v; 2.4 in. RR F/12 w/20mmHy. About 12-15 stars shaped like an arrowhead, reminds me of M103. No background glow.
2174-5	B.N. 7.4 star; 8 in. F/5 w/20mmE. Found while sweeping. *Large*, bright patch, roundish, reminds me of M33. Seen in finderscope. Impressive. Seen in 6 in. scope.
2194	Cl. 9.2v; 2.4 in. RR F/12 w/20mmHy. Faint dim patch of light, use averted vision.
2196	Gal. 12.6p; 8 in. RFL F/5 w/25mmO. Very small, faint, looks like a star, slightly fuzzy. Stellar core with a very thin envelope. Very close to a star of similar brightness. Use averted vision to locate. Smaller but similar brightness to 2207. Seen through a 6 in. scope.
2207	Gal. 11.4p; 8 in. RFL F/5 w/25mmO. Thick elliptical shape, no definite core but slight brightening towards the center. Seen in a 6 in. scope.
2217	Gal. 11.8p; 8 in. RFL F/5 w/25mmO. Small, round with a starlike nucleus. Similar to 2196 but brighter. Seen in a 6 in. scope as brighter than 2280 or 2325, smaller than 2280 but slightly larger than 2325.
2237-9	B.N.; 6 in. RFL F/8 w/25mmO. Known as the Rosette Nebula. The northern part starting at the edge of the cluster (2244) appears bright, being similar in brightness to the faint extended arm of M31. This northern part of the nebula actually fills the eyepiece and sweeping back and forth is a necessity. Impressive.
2244	Cl. 6.2v; 6 in. RFL F/8 w/25mmO. Very bright stars of loose composition fill the eyepiece. This is the cluster "inside" the Rosette Nebula. See 2237-9.
2250	Cl. (?); 6 in. RFL F/6 w/31mmK. Small cluster of about 20 stars in a triangular shape, not compact.
2252	Cl. (?); 6 in. F/6 w/31mmK. Similar to 2250 but slightly smaller in size. About 20 stars with some background glow.
2261	B.N.; 6 in. RFL F/8 w/25mmO. Also known as Hubble's Variable Nebula. Easily seen as a small, bright, fan shaped fuzzy object. At first glance it looks like a miniature comet, complete with a small

Rosette Nebula NGC 2237-9

NGC	DESCRIPTION
	fat tail. Very impressive. As the name implies, this nebula is variable in brightness.
2268	Gal. 12.2p; 6 in. RFL F/8 w/25mmO. Very much extended with no definite core. Larger and slightly brighter than 2300.
2276	Gal. 12.9p; 8 in. Celestron w/25mmK. Easily seen as a large diffuse patch of light, no core seen. In the same field as 2300. Appears brighter than 2300.
2280	Gal. 12.7p; 6 in. RFL F/8 w/25mmO. Slightly elliptical shaped, faint, even brightness throughout, not too small, use averted vision, hard.
2287 (M41)	Cl. 5.1v; 6 in. RFL F/8 w/25mmO. This cluster fills the eyepiece with mostly bright stars. Near the center is an orange star where distinct curved arms of stars radiate from. The overall shape is round. Impressive with low powers. Can be seen with the naked eye.
2300	Gal. 12.2p; 6 in. RFL F/8 w/25mmO. Round, faint patch appearance, use averted vision to locate. Very obvious in an 8 in. Celestron.
2323 (M50)	Cl. 6.9v; 2.4 in. RR F/12 w/20mmHy. Smaller and not as bright as

NGC	DESCRIPTION
	M41, but otherwise similar. At first glance a line of stars appear to enter the cluster from the top left. This line eventually fades into the background as other fainter stars appear. This cluster contains a red star close to its edge. Visually M50 appears as a bright, dense concentration in the Milky Way.
2325	Gal. 12.9p; 6 in. RFL F/8 w/25mmO. Small, faint elliptical, even brightness throughout. Slightly smaller and brighter than 2280.
2336	Gal. 11.0p; 8 in. RFL F/5 w/25mmO. Large, round with a bright fuzzy core. Reminds me of a miniature M33 but with less detail.
2339	Gal. 12.5v; 8 in. RFL F/5 w/25mmO. Bright, large and very easy. Reminds me of M1 but with squared off corners. Also seen with a 6 in. RFL F/8 w/25mmO but was called "hard to see" and could be missed while sweeping.
2360	Cl. 9.5v; 2.4 in. RR F/12 w/20mmHy. Brighter than NGC 2362, almost fills the field of view. About 30 stars with five bright ones. It has a rectangular shape with the top opened. The stars are concentrated in groups. Seen in the 5x finder as a patch of light.
2362	Cl. 10.5v; 2.4 in. RR F/12 w/20mmHy. Very small tight group of stars. A large bright star is centered in this cluster near its top. About ten stars in this cluster with the bright star overshadowing them.
2371-2	Pl.Nb. 13.0 neb/13.3 star; 10 in. RFL F/5.5 w/16.3mmKo. Obvious pale green nebula. Small with two bright nodules almost in contact. Reminds me of M76. 10.2mmO—Western nodule slightly brighter than eastern nodule. A slight wedge of darkness separates the two nodules. Also seen with a 6 in. RFL F/8 w/25mmO.
2392	Pl.Nb. 8.3 neb/10.5 star; 10 in. RFL F/5.5 w/16.3mmKo. Very bright large, round, blue planetary with a star at the center. Outer shell is large and diffuse. Looks like a blue snowball. Also seen with a 6 in. RFL F/8 w/25mmO.
2403	Gal. 8.9v; 8 in. RFL F/5 w/16.3mmKo. Irregular elliptical, faint starlike nucleus with a large envelope. Two "bright" stars of similar brightness, one on each side of the nucleus. 10.2mmO—Mottling seen. Also seen with a 3-1/2 in. Questar and it appeared as a fuzzy patch of light with a 7 x 50 pair of binoculars.
2422 (M47)	Cl. 4.4v; 8 in. RFL F/5 w/16.3mmKo. Irregular shaped cluster with several "bright stars scattered throughout. Five "bright" stars trailing away from M47 in a northward direction, leading to the open cluster NGC 2423. Through the 8 in. scope, this trail of stars appears to be part of M47. Both M47 and 2423 are in the same field. With a 3-1/2 in. Questar the trail of stars appear only as background stars. Basicly M47 is less dense than M46, and has fewer stars. The stars in M47 are brighter than those in M46.
2423	Cl. 6.9v; 8 in. RFL F/5 w/16.3mmKo. Smaller and fainter than M47,

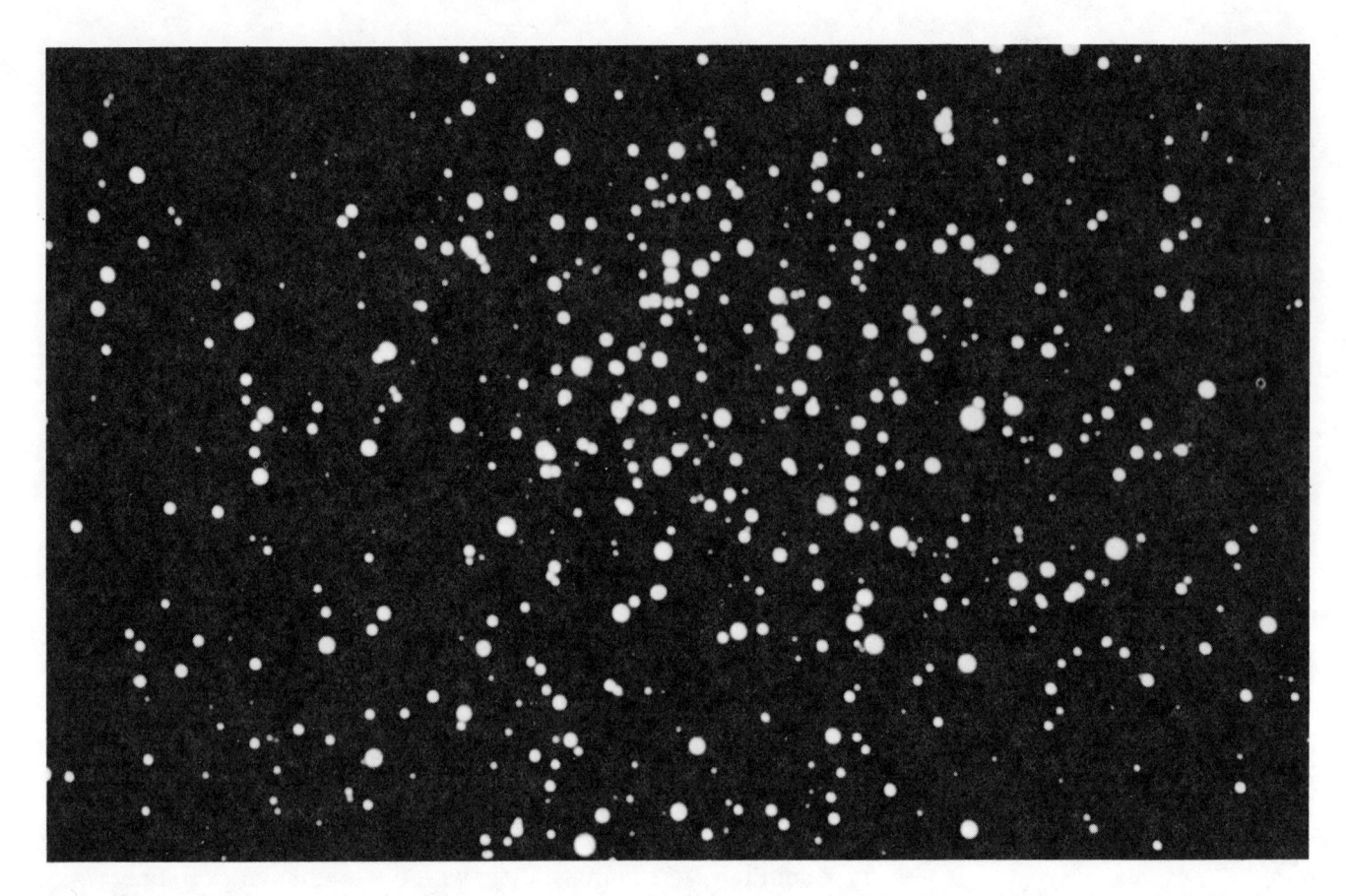

NGC 2437 (M46)

NGC	DESCRIPTION
	round, even distribution throughout.
2425	Cl.; 8 in. RFL F/5 w/16.3mmKo. Found in the Revised NGC of Non Stellar Astronomical Objects. Not listed in the Atlas of the Heavens or Nortons Star Atlas. Located between M46 and M47. A very poor and small group of stars somewhat arrow shaped. Many faint stars give this cluster a slight background glow.
2437 (M46)	Cl. 6.0v; 8 in. RFL F/5 w/16.3mmKo. Fills almost one-third the field of view. Uniformly packed with stars of similar brightness, no background glow. Also seen with a 3-1/2 in. Questar. Planetary Nebula 2438 involved with M46. M46 is visible in 7 x 50 binoculars.
2438	Pl.Nb. 13.3 neb/16.8 star; 8 in. RFL F/5 w/16.3mmKo. Very easy to see, medium sized, round and pale green. Using a 3-1/2 in. Questar, knowing where to look, the planetary nebula was seen as a small pale green disk of uniform brightness. An 8 in. Celestron w/16.3mmKo showed the planetary as definitely ring shaped with a dark center.
2440	Pl.Nb. 11.7 neb/16.5 star; 8 in. RFL F/5 w/16mmKo. Small but bright, bluish-white disk with a fuzzy outer edge. Has a snowball appearance. Not seen in a 3-1/2 in. Questar at 40 power.

NGC	DESCRIPTION
2447 (M93)	Cl. 6.0; 8 in. RFL F/5 w/16mmKo. Small, irregular shaped, compact group of stars with two brighter stars. Approximately; 30 stars. Much smaller than M46 or M47. Seen in a 10 x 40 finderscope as a small patch of light.
2452	Pl.Nb. 12.6 neb/19.0 star; 8 in. RFL F/5 w/16mmKo. Located south of cluster NGC 2453. Very small, round, faint, close to a small triangle of slightly brighter stars. In the same field but not close to 2453.
2453	Op.Cl. 9.4 mag; 8 in. RFL F/5.5 w/16mmKo, 25mmO; (16mm). Small, irregular shaped, compact group, a few individual stars seen, hazy background. 25mm—Seen as an irregular shaped, hazy patch.
2467	B.N.; 8 in. RFL F/5 w/16mmKo. Large, oval shaped, bright nebula with one bright star off center. This nebula reminds me of a brighter version of the Merope nebula (the bright star being in the wrong place). This nebula was seen in a 3-1/2 in. Questar as a patch of light.
2477	Cl. 5.7; 8 in. RFL F/5 w/16mmKo. Atlas of the Heavens Catalogue lists it as a possible Globular. It appeared fairly round, compact with stars of similar brightness. Large and impressive with about 50—60 stars. On the northern edge is a smaller more compact area. Seen in 10 x 40 finder.
2482	Cl. 8.7; 8 in. RFL F/5 w/16mmKo. About 25 stars, medium sized, stars of similar brightness. Has a definite starfish shape. Less compact than M46 or M93. Seen in 10 x 40 finderscope as a small group of stars.
2547	Cl. 5.1; 8 in. RFL F/5 w/16mmKo. Approximately; 40—50 stars loosely scattered throughout the field. No bright stars.
2548 (M48)	Cl. 5.3; 6 in. RFL F/8 w/25mmO. Uniform cluster with about 40—50 stars of similar brightness. A loose cluster with no general shape. Seen with a pair of 7 x 50 binoculars as a large patch of light, easy.
2632 (M44)	Op.Cl. 3.7; 6 in. RFL F/8 w/25mmO. Field of view too small to appreciate cluster. Four—five very bright stars with many dimmer stars. Easy naked-eye object.
2655	Gal. 10.7v; 8 in. RFL F/5 w/16mmKo. Round, bright with a greater brighter middle, envelope easy, no mottling. Seen with a 3-1/2 in. Questar w/40x.
2672	Gal. 12.2v; 8 in. RFL F/5 w/16mmKo. Round, bright core with a "thin" envelope, easy.
2681	Gal. 10.4v; 6 in. RFL F/8 w/25mmO. Round, bright core but smaller and fainter than 2841.
2682 (M67)	Op.Cl. 6.1; 2.4 in. RR w/20mm. Very tight ball of stars, about the

NGC	DESCRIPTION
	same size as M103. Fainter than M50, with the stars about the same magnitude.
2683	Gal. 9.6v; 6 in. RFL F/8 w/25mmO. Round, slightly brighter core, "thin" outer envelope, has globular cluster appearance.
2715	Gal. 11.9v; 8 in. RFL F/5 w/16mmKo. Elliptical shaped, even brightness throughout gives it a "patchlike appearance," no core seen, longer than 2655.
2748	Gal. 11.4v; 8 in. RFL F/5 w/25mmO. Small, bright, very much extended, bright core.
2763	Gal. 12.6p; 6 in. RFL F/8 w/25mmO. Even brightness throughout gives it a patch appearance, extended with a brighter tip on eastern edge (use averted vision), larger than 2781.
2775	Gal. 10.7v; 6 in. RFL F/8 w/25mmO. Round with an envelope and a bright core. Reminds me of NGC 1964, only larger.
2781	Gal. 11.7v; 6 in. RFL F/8 w/25mmO. Small, faint, round with a starlike nucleus, envelope seen with averted vision. Could be mistaken for a star, at first.
2784	Gal. 11.8p; 8 in. RFL F/5 w/25mmO. Bright core, smaller in overall size to NGC 2815, extending arms (edge on) similar to NGC 2835.
2792	Pl.Nb. 13.5n; 10 in. RFL F/5.5 w/16mmKo. Very small, round gray-green disk, even brightness, no central star or dark area seen. 25mm—Appeared stellar. Also seen a stellar in an 8 in. RFL F/5 w/25mm ocular.
2811	Gal. 11.7v; 6 in. RFL F/8 w/25mmO. Small, fuzzy with a brighter nucleus, edge on with a very small, thin envelope, easy.
2815	Gal. 12.9p; 8 in. RFL F/5 w/25mmO. Large, round, even brightness throughout, near bright star, easy.
2832	Gal. 13.5p; 6 in. RFL F/8 w/25mmO. Round, faint, smaller than NGC 2683, thin shell with a brighter core.
2835	Gal. 12.0p; 8 in. RFL F/8 w/25mmO. Medium sized with a very bright core, extended arms are easy to see. Reminds me of a miniature M31.
2841	Gal. 9.3v; 6 in. RFL F/8 w/25mmO. Medium sized, small fuzzy core, very much extended arms. Bright star in western arm near the tip.
2848	Gal. 12.8p; 6 in. RFL F/8 w/25mmO. Small, round with a slightly brighter core, thin envelope, globular cluster appearance, easy.
2855	Gal. 12.2v; 6 in. RFL F/8 w/25mmO. Round, small brighter nucleus appears starlike with averted vision, globular cluster appearance.
2859	Gal. 10.7v; 8 in. RFL F/5 w/16mmKo. Small, round, with a brighter

NGC	DESCRIPTION
	core, thin envelope, also seen in the 6 in., easy.
2865	Gal. 12.5p; 8 in. RFL F/5 w/25mmO. Small, round, bright core with a thin envelope, could easily be mistaken for a star. Not seen in the 6 in.
2889	Gal. 12.4p; 6 in. RFL F/8 w/25mmO. Faint, round with no brighter core, easy. Reminds me of a miniature Owl Nebula (M97). Interesting.
2903	Gal. 9.1v; 6 in. RFL F/8 w/25mmO. Bright, very large, thick body with very much extended envelope, bright core, easy and impressive.
2964	Gal. 11.0v; 6 in. RFL F/8 w/25mmO. Round, even brightness throughout, brighter than NGC 2968 and in the same field. With a 10.2mmO a brighter core was seen, easy.
2968	Gal. 11.9v; 6 in. RFL F/8 w/25mmO. Round, even brightness throughout gives it a patch appearance, smaller than NGC 2964. With a 10.2mmO the "western" arm appeared brighter than the "eastern," as if there may be a faint star in it.
2974	Gal. 11.0v; 6 in. RFL F/8 w/25mmO. Faint, extended faint envelope (arms), no core, small.
2992	Gal. 13.0p; 10 in. RFL F/6 w/16mmKo. In same field as NGC 2993. 2992 appears longer and slightly brighter than 2993, brighter core, thin outer envelope. It was also seen in the 6 in., use averted vision at first.
2993	Gal. 13.9p; 10 in. RFL F/6 w/16mmKo. Small, round, fainter than NGC 2992, even brightness throughout. Also seen in the 6 in. with the help of averted vision.
2997	Gal. 11.0p; 8 in. RFL F/5 w/25mmO. Large, bright, face on with one star involved, slightly brighter core seen, easy.
3003	Gal. 12.7v; 8 in. RFL F/5 w/16mmKo. Large, edge on, even brightness throughout with a much thicker core area. Same field as NGC 3021.
3021	Gal. 11.7v; 8 in. RFL F/5 w/16mmKo. Round, close to a star, possible slight brightening near core, smaller than NGC 3003. Same field as 3003.
3031 (M81)	Gal. 7.9 mag; 8 in. RFL F/5 w/16mmKo. Wider, larger and brighter than M82. Fuzzy edges with a larger and brighter core than M82, also in the same field. 6 in. RFL F/8 w/9mm—It appears to have a dark streak coming up from the center, as if cut in two from the bottom up. This was glimpsed with averted vision.
3034 (M82)	Gal. 8.8 mag; 8 in. RFL F/5 w/16mmKo—Thin and bright but longer than M81. Very elongated with a possible dark lane.

NGC	DESCRIPTION
3034 (M82) Con't	10 in. RFL F/6 w/16mmKo. Very bright, very large, edge on, one very dark band through thickness of galaxy, near core. Two others glimpsed with averted vision on either side of Primary Dark Band; but along the same axis. Very bright core, very bright envelope, elliptical. Impressive.
3044	Gal. 12.6p; 10 in. RFL F/6 w/16mmG. Very much extended, even brightness throughout, average sized, sharp edges, easy. Seen with the 6 in.
3054	Gal. 12.6p; 8 in. RFL F/5 w/25mmO. Bright, elliptical, even brightness throughout, no core, very close to a "bright" star.
3079	Gal. 11.2v; 6 in. RFL F/8 w/25mmO. Very much extended, thin, no core, even brightness throughout, easy.
3109	Gal. 11.2p; 8 in. RFL F/5 w/25mmO. Very much extended with a thick core area, even brightness throughout, two stars involved in envelope.
3115	Gal. 9.3v; 6 in. RFL F/8 w/25mmO. Bright, edge on with a bright core, long arms, very easy.
3132	Pl.Nb. 8.2 neb/10.6 star; 10 in. RFL F/6 w/25mm; 12mmKo—(25). Very bright condensed but not stellar core, blue-white with a very large elliptical shaped diffuse envelope that is evenly textured. 12mm—Uncertain as to any dark space between the very bright core and the outer envelope. Reminds me of NGC 40 only with a brighter core. Also seen in a 6 in. F/8 scope w/25mm ocular.
3158	Gal. 13.1p; 6 in. RFL F/8 w/25mmO. Faint, small, round, starlike nucleus, faint outer envelope. Could be mistaken for a star.
3162	Gal. 12.3p; 6 in. RFL F/8 w/25mmO. Faint, patch appearance, slightly brighter and larger than NGC 3177.
3166	Gal. 11.4v; 6 in. RFL F/8 w/25mmO. Small, elliptical shape, bright core, same field as NGC 3169, easy.
3169	Gal. 11.7v; 6 in. RFL F/8 w/25mmO. Small, elliptical shape, bright core, similar to NGC 3166 which is in the same field.
3172	Gal. 14.9p; 10 in. RFL F/5.5 w/16mmKo. Use averted vision, seen as a small, very faint, round patch.
3177	Gal. 12.8p; 10 in. RFL F/6 w/16mmKo. Small, round, bright core, looks like a globular cluster, with its thin outer envelope. Just outside the field are three other galaxies, NGC 3178, 3190 and 3193.
3184	Gal. 9.6v; 6 in. RFL F/8 w/25mmO. Roundish, diffuse, fairly large, no core, even brightness throughout. One star seen near northern edge. With averted vision a possible starlike nucleus is seen.
3185	Gal. 12.9p; 10 in. RFL F/6 w/16mmG. In the same field as NGC

NGC	DESCRIPTION
	3187, 3190 and 3193. Largest of the group, round, small with a starlike nucleus, faint envelope, longest and farthest from the group. Seen with the 6 in.
3187	Gal. 13.0v; 10 in. RFL F/6 w/16mmG. Not listed in Skalnate Pleso Atlas. Faint, patchlike, may be extended, even brightness throughout. Not seen with the 6 in.
3190	Gal. 11.3v; 10 in. RFL F/6 w/16mmG. Brightest of the group (3185, 3187, 3190 and 3193), very much extended with a bright core. Seen with the 6 in.
3193	Gal. 11.5v; 10 in. RFL F/6 w/16mmG. Round, small with a bright nucleus gives it a globular cluster appearance. Seen in the 6 in. but envelope needs averted vision at first.
3201	Gb.Cl. 7.4p; 6 in. RFL F/6 w/16mmG. Very large, very bright, dense core with many individual stars seen near the edges. Reminds me of a miniature Omega Centauri, impressive.
3213	Gal. 14.3p; 10 in. RFL F/6 w/16mmKo. Not listed in Skalnate Pleso Atlas. Small, patchlike, even brightness throughout, slightly brighter core, very faint. Not seen in the 8 in.
3222	Gal. 14.5p; 10 in. RFL F/6 w/16mmKo. Not listed in Skalnate Pleso Atlas. Small, patchlike with a brighter core. Knowing exactly where to look, by comparing the fields of the 10 in. and an 8 in., it was seen in the 8 in. scope, use averted vision.
3226	Gal. 11.4v; 10 in. RFL F/6 w/16mmKo. Elliptical, bright nucleus, thin envelope, *very* close to NGC 3227. Seen in the 6 in.
3227	Gal. 11.4v; 10 in. RFL F/6 w/16mmKo. Elliptical with a starlike nucleus. Larger than NGC 3226 but of the same brightness. In fact, NGC 3226 and 3227 appear as one galaxy separated by a dark lane or area. Seen in the 6 in. although separation of the two galaxies is more difficult.
3242	Pl.Nb. 9.0 neb/11.4 star; 6 in. RFL F/8 w/25mmO. Very bright, disk shaped, pale blue, no central star seen.
3245	Gal. 11.2v; 8 in. RFL F/5 w/16mmKo. Easily seen as an elliptical patch, brighter core with outer envelope easy. Seen in the 6 in.
3254	Gal. 12.2v; 6 in. RFL F/8 w/25mmO. South of a bright star in the same field. Diffuse with a slightly brighter core, faint extended envelope.
3277	Gal. 12.0v; 6 in. RFL F/8 w/25mmO. Round, slightly fainter and smaller than average, possible brighter core with averted vision. NGC 3277 forms a right triangle with two faint stars.
3294	Gal. 11.4v; 6 in. RFL F/8 w/25mmO. Elliptical, faint, no core, patch appearance.

NGC	DESCRIPTION
3338	Gal. 11.3p; 6 in. RFL F/8 w/25mmO. Much brighter than NGC 3346, also slightly larger. Elliptical with a possibly slight brightening near the center. Star very close to western arm near tip.
3344	Gal. 10.4v; 6 in. RFL F/8 w/25mmO. Small, diffuse, possible starlike nucleus, thin outer envelope, elliptical, brighter star touching outer envelope, fainter star inside envelope.
3346	Gal. 11.7v; 6 in. RFL F/8 w/25mmO. Roundish patch, no nucleus, small, easy.
3351 (M95)	Gal. 10.4 mag; 8 in. Celestron F/10 w/25mm. Round, bright fuzzy, brighter core gives it a globular cluster look.
3367	Gal. 11.9p; 6 in. RFL F/8 w/25mmO. Round, patch appearance with no brighter core. Dimmer than NGC 3377.
3368 (M96)	Gal. 9.1 mag; 8 in. Celestron F/10 w/25mm. Round, slightly larger than M95 but with a brighter core, easy.
3377	Gal. 10.5v; 6 in. RFL F/8 w/25mmO. Round, patch appearance with a brighter core, easy.
3379 (M105)	Gal. 9.2v; 6 in. RFL F/8 w/25mmO. Brightest of three in the field, NGC 3379, 3384 and 3389. Very bright, round with a brighter core, easy.
3384	Gal. 10.2v; 6 in. RFL F/8 w/25mmO. Round with a very bright core, very little envelope seen.
3389	Gal. 12.5v; 6 in. RFL F/8 w/25mmO. Faint, may be round, has fuzzy patchlike appearance, use averted vision.
3395	Gal. 12.0v; 10 in. RFL F/5 w/10.2mmO. Very close to NGC 3396, somewhat extended, small sized, no brighter core seen, a little brighter than 3396. Also seen in the 6 in. F/8 w/25mmO.
3396	Gal. 12.7v; 10 in. RFL F/5w/10.2mmO. Round with no brighter core, small, a little fainter than 3395. It does appear a little smaller and thinner than 3395. Also seen in the 6 in. scope.
3412	Gal. 10.4v; 6 in. RFL F/8 w/25mmO. Elliptical with a brighter core, fainter than 3379, easy.
3413	Gal. 13.0p; 10 in. RFL F/5 w/10.2mmO. Elongated with no brighter core, easy. Not seen with the 6 in. F/8.
3414	Gal. 11.0v; 6 in. RFL F/8 w/25mmO. Faint, small, round, with averted vision a slightly brighter core is seen.
3423	Gal. 11.5p; 8 in. Celestron w/40mmK. Round, even brightness throughout, easy.
3424	Gal. 13.2p; 8 in. RFL F/5 w/16mmKo. Easily seen as a patch of light about 1/2 the diameter and fainter than NGC 3430, even

NGC	DESCRIPTION
	brightness throughout. Seen in the same field as NGC 3430. Averted vision not needed. Seen through the 6 in. using averted vision.
3430	Gal. 12.0v; 8 in. RFL F/8 w/16mmKo. Elliptical, fairly bright patch, no bright core. Just outside the field from NGC 3395 and 3396. About same size as both galaxies (3395 and 3396) combined but a little brighter. Seen in 6 in.
3432	Gal. 11.4v; 8 in. RFL F/5 w/16mmKo. Somewhat brighter than expected, elongated, very thick with the edges as thick as the middle, almost rectangular shaped, two stars in envelope one at each extreme edge.
3442	Gal. 13.0p; 10 in. RFL F/6 w/31mmK. Small, elliptical, even brightness throughout. Slightly larger than and similar in brightness to NGC 3413. Smaller than NGC 3395, 3396, 3430 and 3424. Not seen in 6 in. scope.
3486	Gal. 11.2v; 8 in. RFL F/5 w/16mmKo. Considerably bright, round, small patch easily seen, mottling suspected. Also seen in the 6 in. scope.
3504	Gal. 10.9v; 8 in. RFL F/5 w/16mmKo. Appears twice the size of NGC 3512, both in the same field, with averted vision a slight brightening in the middle was seen. Seen in the 6 in. scope.
3511	Gal. 11.9p; 6 in. RFL F/8 w/25mmO. In same field as NGC 3513, 3511 the longer of the two, elongated, sharp edges, even brightness throughout, easy.
3512	Gal. 11.7v; 8 in. RFL F/5 w/16mmKo. Elliptical shaped, patch appearance, appears slightly fainter than NGC 3504. Seen in the 6 in. scope.
3513	Gal. 12.0p; 6 in. RFL F/8 w/25mmO. Small, round, even brightness throughout, fainter than NGC 3511.
3556 (M108)	Gal. 10.7v; 6 in. RFL F/8 w/25mmO. Large, fainter than M81, very much extended, a hint of a dark lane, bright core seen near the northern edge of center. Just outside the field of M97.
3587 (M97)	Pl.Nb. 12.0 neb/14.3 star; 8 in. RFL F/5 w/16mmKo. Very large, round, bright, one "eye" definite, the second "eye" only suspected, impressive.
3593	Gal. 11.3v; 6 in. RFL F/8 w/25mmO. Elongated, faint, no brighter core, fainter than NGC 3626.
3623 (M65)	Gal. 9.3 mag; 8 in. RFL F/5 w/16mmKo. Bright, somewhat extended, nucleus slightly more conspicuous than M66. Both M65 and M66 in same field.
3627 (M66)	Gal. 8.4 mag; 8 in. RFL F/5 w/16mmKo. Slightly brighter than M65, elliptical with a brighter nucleus. Obvious star seen just outside

NGC 3556 (M108)

NGC 3992 (M109)

NGC	DESCRIPTION
	envelope to the northwest.
3628	Gal. 10.9v; 6 in. RFL F/8 w/25mmO. Fainter but much longer than M65 or M66, very much extended, uneven texture, no bright core.
3640	Gal. 10.7v; 6 in. RFL F/8 w/25mmO. Round with a much brighter core and a starlike nucleus, globular cluster in appearance.
3681	Gal. 12.4v; 8 in. Celestron w/40mmK. Round, no bright core, fainter than NGC 3684 and 3686 also in the same field.
3684	Gal. 12.4v; 8 in. Celestron w/40mmK. Slightly elongated, patchlike, no bright core.
3686	Gal. 11.4v; 8 in. Celestron w/40mmK. Brightest and largest of all three in the field, no bright core. See NGC 3681 and 3684.
3726	Gal. 10.8p; 10 in. RFL F/5.5 w/16mmKo. Large, patch appearance, elongated with a star on western edge, averted vision shows a brighter core off center. Similar in overall size to NGC 3877 but 3726 is fuller and less elongated.
3782	Gal. 13.0p; 10 in. RFL F/5.5 w/16mmKo. Faintest and smallest of three (NGC 3769, 3782 and 3726), two faint stars seen, one on each arm sort of extending the nebula on its ends, elongated. Averted vision helps to find it, then not needed, patch appearance.
3877	Gal. 10.9; 10 in. RFL F/5.5 w/16mmKo. Edge on galaxy, medium sized, much thicker middle, gradually brighter middle, possibility of mottling, easy. Seen in the 6 in. scope.
3893	Gal. 11.3; 10 in. RFL F/5.5 w/16mmKo. In same field as NGC 3896. 3893 is the brighter of the two also larger of the two. Round with an almost starlike center. Brighter but smaller than NGC 3877, easy. Also seen in the 6 in. scope.
3896	Gal. 14.0; 10 in. RFL F/5.5 w/16mmKo. Seen with averted vision as a small patch of light. Not seen in 6 in. scope. Not listed in Skalnate Pleso Atlas.
3949	Gal. 11.0; 6 in. RFL F/8 w/25mmO. Round, small, even brightness throughout. Smaller and fainter than NGC 3893.
3976	Gal. 12.4p; 10 in. RFL F/5.5 w/16mmKo. Faint, round and small with a much brighter middle.
3981	Gal. 12.7p; 10 in. RFL F/5.5 w/24mmKo. Slightly fainter than NGC 4027 but about the same size with no brighter core, north—south orientation. Faint star seen on eastern edge near center of galaxy, patchlike and thinner than 4027. Also seen in 6 in. RFL F/5 with 16mm ocular.
3985	Gal. 12.9p; 10 in. RFL F/5.5 w/16mmKo. Slightly fainter and smaller than NGC 3983, a starlike core is seen with averted

NGC	DESCRIPTION
	vision, elliptical.
3992 (M109)	Gal. 10.8 mag; 8 in. Celestron F/10 w/16mmKo. A round condensed very bright core in which no mottling was detected. The outer envelope was fairly large and extended southwest—northeast but was fainter than expected. Near the northern border, not far from the nucleus, there is an obvious star.
4027	Gal. 11.6p; 8 in. RFL F/5 w/25mmO. Same field as NGC 4038 but much smaller, similar brightness, elliptical with a slight brightening towards the center. Seen in 6 in. scope.
4030	Gal. 11.0; 10 in. RFL F/5.5 w/16mmKo. Round, much brighter towards the center. In the 6 in. scope it looked somewhat like a tightly packed (unresolved) globular cluster.
4038	Gal. 11.0; 8 in. RFL F/5 w/16mmKo. Round with a dark lane running 3/4 of the way through the center, giving the galaxy an overall appearance of a fat "U" shaped object, southern portion of "U" appears brighter and slightly larger than northern side. Seen in 6 in. scope.
4045	Gal. 12.8p; 10 in. RFL F/5.5 w/16mmKo. Round patch of light, even brightness throughout, easy. Not seen in 6 in.
4100	Gal. 11.9; 10 in. RFL F/5.5 w/16mmKo. Brighter and larger than NGC 4248, elliptical shaped, slight brightening towards the center, easy.
4116	Gal. 12.3p; 6 in. RFL F/8 w/25mmO. Slightly fainter than NGC 4123 in the same field, elliptical, even brightness throughout.
4123	Gal. 11.8p; 6 in. RFL F/8 w/25mmO. Elliptical, patch with a slightly brighter center.
4144	Gal. 12.4p; 10 in. RFL F/5.5 w/16mmKo. Very much extended, medium sized, slightly brighter middle, much thicker in the center, bright star outside envelope near western tip.
4147	Gb.Cl. 9.4; 8 in. RFL F/5 w/16mmKo. Bright, very condensed nucleus, round, a few individual stars seen on the outer edges, smaller than M53.
4151	Gal. 11.6; 6 in. RFL F/8 w/25mmO. Round with a globular cluster appearance, round with a brighter nucleus and a starlike center.
4190	Gal. 13.2p; 10 in. RFL F/5.5 w/16mmKo. In same field as NGC 4214, faint, round, even brightness throughout, smaller than NGC 4214.
4192 (M98)	Gal. 10.7; 6 in. RFL F/8 w/25mmO. Very much extended, even brightness throughout with one edge appearing very sharp, no brighter core seen, easy.
4203	Gal. 11.0; 6 in. RFL F/8 w/25mmO. Round, greater brighter middle,

NGC	DESCRIPTION
	somewhat smaller than average, two stars just outside reach of envelope, bright star in same field.
4214	Gal. 10.3; 10 in. RFL F/5.5 w/16mmKo. Medium sized object, slightly elongated with a bright core. Also seen in 6 in. F/8 scope.
4215	Gal. 12.8p; 10 in. RFL F/5.5 w/16mmKo. Small galaxy, compact, much brighter middle, elliptical. Easily found while sweeping.
4217	Gal. 11.9p; 10 in. RFL F/5.5 w/16mmKo. Very thin, long galaxy, close to two obvious stars, even brightness throughout galaxy, no brighter core seen. Averted vision helps with the long thin extensions.
4220	Gal. 11.7; 10 in. RFL F/5.5 w/16mmKo. In the same field as NGC 4248. Slightly larger than 4248, elongated patch of light, slight brightening near the center, easy.
4224	Gal. 12.9p; 10 in. RFL F/5.5 w/16mmKo. Larger than NGC 4233 or 4235. Definite patch appearance, small and faint.
4226	Gal. 14.4p; 10 in. RFL F/5.5 w/16mmKo. This galaxy is not listed in the Skalnate Pleso Atlas. Slightly east of NGC 4217, a small, round fuzzy patch of light, fainter than 4217, averted vision helps.
4231	Gal. 14.5p; 10 in. RFL F/5.5 w/16mmKo. Not listed in Skalnate Pleso Atlas. Seen close to NGC 4232, it appeared stellar but was identified, using 4232 as a guide. See NGC 4232.
4232	Gal. 14.6p; 10 in. RFL F/5.5 w/16mmKo. In the same field as NGC 4231. At first both NGC 4231 and 4232 appear to be just three faint stars, in the same field but not close to NGC 4248. During moments of good seeing, one of these three stars appears as a faint but distinct, small patch of light. A second star may also be involved.
4233	Gal. 13.0p; 10 in. RFL F/5.5 w/16mmKo. Seen in same field as 4224 and 4235. Smallest and faintest of group, patch appearance.
4235	Gal. 12.6p; 10 in. RFL F/5.5 w/16mmKo. South of 4224 and 4233, irregular shaped patch appearance, somewhat edge on. Similar in brightness to NGC 4224, NGC 4235 = IC3098.
4236	Gal. 12.4v; 10 in. RFL F/5.5 w/16mmKo. Large and very much elongated, even brightness throughout. Similar in appearance to NGC 4945 as both were patch like, but 4236 appeared more like a fine grained object than a nebulous one. It looked almost as if it were a detached portion of the Zodical light, texture wise! It appeared brighter than the listed 12.4 magnitude might suggest, also it did not appear larger than NGC 4945. Five stars, of similar magnitude, partly surrounded this galaxy on its northern portion.

NGC	DESCRIPTION
FIG. #4	NGC 4236
	10 in. F/5.5 with 16mm ocular

4244	Gal. 11.9v; 10 in. RFL F/5.5 w/16mmKo/25mmO. 25mm— Reminds me of NGC 4565, but smaller and slightly dimmer. Very elongated, thickening towards the center, no bright core no stars in the envelope. 16mm—Elongated approximately; east—west. Near the eastern tip just above the extension is a fairly obvious star. The north—west edge is sharper than the south—east edge. Slight gradual brightening seen off center. Fills approximately; 1/4 field of view. Impressive! Seen in 6 in. F/8 scope w/25mm ocular.
4246	Gal. 14.0p; 10 in. RFL F/5.5 w/16mmKo. Just north and slightly east of NGC 4215. Not in Skalnate Pleso. Near limit of the telescope, patch, may be elongated, similar in size to 4224, averted vision necessary.
4248	Gal. 13.9p; 10 in. RFL F/5.5 w/16mmKo. Not listed in the Skalnate Pleso. It's located about 1/4 of the way from M106 to NGC 4220. This galaxy is in the same field with M106. It was a small fuzzy patch of light, shape not certain but seen without averted vision.
4254 (M99)	Gal. 10.1v; 6 in. RFL F/8 w/25mmO. Larger and brighter than M98, slightly elongated with a brighter core.
4258 (M106)	Gal. 8.6v; 10 in. RFL F/5.5 w/16mmKo. Extremely large, very bright with a very bright compact center. Very much extended approximately; north—south. Outer envelope fuzzy and large. Near one extension is a faint star, almost touching the envelope.
4260	Gal. 12.7p; 10 in. RFL F/5.5 w/16mmKo. Small irregular shaped object with a greater brighter middle, easy.
4261	Gal. 10.3v; 10 in. RFL F/5.5 w/16mmKo. Slightly brighter than 4260, round with a compact brighter center.
4264	Gal. 13.9p; 10 in. RFL F/5.5 w/16mmKo. North of 4261, small round patchlike object with a greater brighter middle. Not in Skalnate Pleso Atlas.

NGC	DESCRIPTION
4268	Gal. 13.9p; 10 in. RFL F/5.5 w/16mmKo. Fainter than NGC 4281, 4270 or 4273, averted vision shows a round shape, patch appearance. Not in Skalnate Pleso.
4270	Gal. 13.3p; 10 in. RFL F/5.5 w/16mmKo. Slightly larger than NGC 4273, round with patch appearance.
4273	Gal. 11.6v; 10 in. RFL F/5.5 w/16mmKo. Brightest of all in the field, small and round with a compact center.
4281	Gal. 11.3v; 10 in. RFL F/5.5 w/16mmKo. Part of a group consisting of 4270, 4268, 4273 and 4300, all fairly close together except for 4300 which is off to one side by itself. NGC 4281 appears smaller than 4270 or 4273, patch appearance with a slightly brighter core.
4290	Gal. 12.7p; 10 in. RFL F/5.5 w/16mmKo. Small, irregular patch of light, even brightness throughout, no brighter core.
4300	Gal. 13.9p; 10 in. RFL F/5.5 w/16mmKo. Smallest and faintest of the group consisting of NGC 4281, 4270, 4268, 4273 and 4300. Not listed in Skalnate Pleso.
4303 (M61)	Gal. 10.1v; 6 in. RFL F/8 w/25mmO. Round, diffuse with a small core, averted vision helps on the small core.
4312	Gal. 12.5p; 10 in. RFL F/5.5 w/16mmKo. Not listed in Skalnate Pleso Atlas. Very obvious in the scope. Very much extended with a thick mid region, a possible slightly brighter core, no definite core seen, about 2/3 the size of M100, just south of M100. An impressive thick edge on galaxy, could be found while sweeping.
4321 (M100)	Gal. 10.6v; 10 in. RFL F/5.5 w/16mmKo. Very large galaxy, the nucleus was condensed and bright. The outer envelope was not perfectly round (face-on). It was quite diffuse and extended quite a distance from the core. No spiral structure was apparent. Both M100 and 4312 were seen in the same field, but at opposite ends. M100 also seen in 6 in. scope.
4346	Gal. 11.6v; 10 in. RFL F/5.5 w/16mmKo. Very small, bright patch of light, no definite shape, slightly brighter towards the center.
4361	Pl.Nb. 10.8 neb/12.8 star; 8 in. RFL F/5 w/10.2mmO. Bright, round, diffuse with irregular edges, central star easily seen. 25mmO— Looks like a fuzzy patch, central star suspected. Seen in a 6 in. scope.
4374 (M84)	Gal. 9.3v; 6 in. RFL F/8 w/25mmO. Very bright, round, looks like an unresolved globular cluster. In the same field as M86, 4388, 4435 and 4438. M84 looks similar to M86.
4382 (M85)	Gal. 9.3v; 6 in. RFL F/8 w/25mmO. Appears round and diffuse with a small stellar nucleus. Reminds me of a comet's nucleus during the early stages.
4388	Gal. 11.7p; 6 in. RFL F/8 w/25mmO. Very much extended, fainter

NGC	DESCRIPTION
	than M84 or M86 but still obvious. Even brightness throughout.
4395	Gal. 10.7p; 10 in. RFL F/6 w/31mmK. Round (face-on), faint, no structure, easy.
4406 (M86)	Gal. 9.7v; 6 in. RFL F/8 w/25mmO. Almost identical to M84. Very bright, round, looks like an unresolved globular cluster, easy.
4435	Gal. 10.3v; 6 in. RFL F/8 w/25mmO. Roundish, diffuse, fainter than M84 and M86 but brighter than 4388. Looks similar to 4438 and both are close together in the field (4435 and 4438).
4438	Gal. 10.8v; 6 in. RFL F/8 w/25mmO. This galaxy looks similar to NGC 4435. Not as round as 4438, diffuse and fainter than M84 and M86 but brighter than 4388.
4448	Gal. 11.4v; 6 in. RFL F/8 w/25mmO. Small and faint, may be elliptical in shape.
4472 (M49)	Gal. 8.6v; 6 in. RFL F/8 w/25mmO. Bright, round with a bright core. Definite globular cluster appearance.
4478	Gal. 10.9v; 6 in. RFL F/8 w/25mmO. In the same field as M87. Small with a brighter core, round. Averted vision helps on outer envelope.
4485	Gal. 11.6v; 10 in. RFL F/5.5 w/16mmKo. In same field as 4490, but smaller and fainter. Round, bright patch of light, no central core seen. Very close to NGC 4490. Seen in 6 in. scope.
4486 (M87)	Gal. 9.2v; 6 in. RFL F/8 w/25mmO. Bright, large with a brighter core, extended outer envelope, looks somewhat elliptical.
4490	Gal. 9.7v; 10 in. RFL F/5.5 w/16mmKo. Very large and bright, very much extended, no central core seen, but there is slight brightening towards the center. In the same field as NGC 4485, but closer to Beta CVn than 4485. Seen in 6 in. scope.
4494	Gal. 9.6v; 8 in. Celestron w/40mmK. Bright and round with definite brightening towards the center, round. Seen in the 6 in. scope.
4501 (M88)	Gal. 10.2v; 6 in. RFL F/8 w/25mmO. Larger than M99, patch of light with a brighter core, extended envelope, easy.
4548 (M91)	Gal. 10.8v; 6 in. RFL F/8 w/25mmO. Slightly smaller than M88. Bright core, extended envelope, elliptical.
4552 (M89)	Gal. 9.5v; 6 in. RFL F/8 w/25mmO. Outside the field from M90. Much brighter core than M90, small and round, averted vision helps on the outer envelope.
4559	Gal. 10.6v; 8 in. Celestron w/40mmK. Irregular shaped patch of light, no bright core, galaxy is situated between two faint stars, one above and one below, easy.

NGC	DESCRIPTION
4562	Gal. 14.5p; 10 in. RFL F/6 w/31mmK. Just below 4565, very faint patch of light, use averted vision, hard.
4565	Gal. 10.2v; 10 in. RFL F/6 w/16.3mmG. Very much extended, edge on galaxy, bright, with a much brighter core, dark lane on southern tip, very straight edges, one of the showpieces of the heavens, impressive! Also seen in a 3-1/2 in. Questar scope.
4569 (M90)	Gal. 10.0v; 6 in. RFL F/8 w/25mmO. Elliptical shaped, bright core, brighter than M88, easy.
4576	Gal. 14.5p; 10 in. RFL F/6 w/31mmK. Round, small with a brighter core, globular cluster appearance, averted vision not needed, brighter than expected.
4579 (M58)	Gal. 9.2v; 8 in. RFL F/5 w/32mmP. Roundish with a definite brighter core, brighter than M59, easy.
4590 (M68)	Gb.Cl. 8.2 mag; 6 in. RFL F/8 w/25mmO. Very bright, fuzzy but no individual stars seen. 12.7mm—Hint of a granular structure. 8 in. Celestron w/12mm—Individual stars seen at cluster's edge.
4594 (M104)	Gal. 8.7v; 10 in. RFL F/5.5 w/16mmKo. Very large and bright, very much extended, dark lane not seen, small condensed bright core, outer edges very straight. Continued viewing of this object seems to bring out subtle detail, impressive. Seen in 6 in. scope.
4618	Gal. 11.7v; 10 in. RFL F/5.5 w/16mmKo. In the same field as NGC 4525 (not shown in Skalnate Pleso), NGC 4618 is brighter than NGC 4625, patchlike appearance. During moments of good seeing, it appears that 4618 is cut in half by a dark lane, but this is not certain! The two galaxies are very close together, the dark lane has nothing to do with their closeness.
4621 (M59)	Gal. 9.6v; 8 in. RFL F/5 w/32mmP. Small, round, bright, brighter core, it appears as a fuzzy "star" with a thin outer envelope.
4625 (IC3675)	Gal. 13.0p; 10 in. RFL F/5.5 w/16mmKo. Very close to NGC 4618, patchlike appearance, no bright core, fainter than 4618, averted vision not needed once found, shape uncertain.
4627	Gal. 13.5p; 10 in. RFL F/6 w/31mmK. Very close to nucleus of NGC 4631, not seen at first, fuzzy smudge appearance use averted vision. Hard!
4631	Gal. 9.3v; 10 in. RFL F/5.5 w/16mmKo. Larger and brighter than NGC 4656 which is in the same field. Extremely large, very much elongated, flat, no brighter core, faint star just outside mid region. Slight mottling suspected (with averted vision) in the thinner of the two extensions.
4639	Gal. 12.1p; 8 in. RFL F/5 w/32mmP. Dimmer than NGC 4654, round, slightly brighter core.
4647	Gal. 12.0p; 8 in. RFL F/5 w/32mmP. Smaller than M60 and fainter,

NGC	DESCRIPTION
	round, very close to M60, no core seen. Dark space between M60 and 4647.
4649 (M60)	Gal. 8.9v; 8 in. RFL F/5 w/32mmP. Bright, round with a bright core, M60 appears brighter than M58, M59 or NGC 4647.
4654	Gal. 11.0p; 8 in. RFL F/5 w/32mmP. Seen edge on, not very large, slightly thicker core area, no bright core, in the same field as NGC 4639, easy.
4656	Gal. 11.2v; 10 in. RFL F/5.5 16mmKo. Smaller than 4631, thin edge on galaxy, central core seen off center, slight brightening seen near this core. In the same field as 4631. Also seen in 6 in. scope.
4736 (M94)	Gal. 7.9v; 10 in. RFL F/5.5 w/16mmKo. Extremely bright elliptical shaped large galaxy with a very bright condensed core, not much detail for amateur scopes. Seen in 6 in. scope and 10 x 40mm finderscope.
4826 (M64)	Gal. 8.8v; 10 in. RFL F/5.5 w/16mmKo. Large, very bright elliptical shaped object. A definite dark area was seen touching and partly surrounding the nucleus. The nucleus itself was a very bright, much condensed area. This dark area is small but averted vision is not needed. This dark area was also seen in the 8 in. scope. Galaxy also seen in 3-1/2 in. Questar but dark area was not seen.
4868	Gal. 13.1p; 10 in. RFL F/5.5 w/16mmKo. Fainter than 4914 but brighter than 4893 (much brighter). NGC 4914 (12.7) NGC 4893 (15.6p) and NGC 4868 were all in the same field. NGC 4868 was the closest of the three to a bright star. It had a patchlike appearance, even brightness throughout with a dim star on its northwest edge, small outer envelope, easy.
4893	Gal. 15.6p; 10 in. RFL F/5.5 w/16mmKo. Faintest of the three in the field (see NGC 4868). Slightly larger than 4914 or 4868, definite patch appearance, found with averted vision at first but then held steady with direct vision. Much brighter than expected.
4914	Gal. 12.7p; 10 in. RFL F/5.5 w/16mmKo. The brightest of the trio (see NGC 4868) also the farthest from the bright star. Round with a stellar core, it also had a small outer envelope similar to 4868.
4945	Gal. 9.2p; 10 in. RFL F/5.5 w/16mmKo. Very large, very much elongated, faint, even textured patch with definite edges, with averted vision it may be "fine grained." Also seen in 8 in. scope. See NGC 4976.
4976	Gal. 11.6p; 10 in. RFL F/5.5 w/16mmKo. In the same field and very close to NGC 4945, elliptical with a brighter middle, smaller than 4945. Also seen in 8 in. scope.
5005	Gal. 9.8v; 10 in. RFL F/5.5 w/16mmKo. Seen in the same field as NGC 5033. Brighter than 5033, elongated with a much brighter middle, long faint extensions, almost starlike nucleus *inside* a

NGC	DESCRIPTION
	bright core, mottled, large and easy. Also seen in a 6 in. F/8 scope.
5014	Gal. 13.5p; 10 in. RFL F/5.5 w/16mmKo. Not in Skalnate Pleso, Due south of NGC 5033, small, faint galaxy first seen with averted vision, patch appearance, thin with an elongated envelope, can be seen with direct vision.
5024 (M53)	Gb.Cl. 7.6v; 8 in. RFL F/5 w/10.2mmO. Large, bright and round with outer portions resolved into individual stars. Center is a blaze of fire! Also seen in 6 in. scope.
5033	Gal. 10.3v; 10 in. RFL F/5.5 w/16mmKo. Slightly smaller and fainter than 5005, small compact bright center, envelope elongated in an east—west direction, easy. Also seen in a 6 in. F/8 telescope.
5053	Gb.Cl. 10.5p; 8 in. RFL F/5 w/16mmKo. Large, faint and round, a few individual stars are seen near the edge. Larger than M53. Also seen with a 3-1/2 in. Questar.
5055 (M63)	Gal. 9.5v; 6 in. RFL F/8 w/25mmp. Elliptical, patchlike object, gradually brightening towards the center, easy.
5107	Gal. 13.7p; 10 in. RFL F/5.5 w/16mmKo. Not listed in Skalnate Pleso. In the same field as NGC 5112. Fainter and smaller than 5112, elongated, patch appearance, even brightness throughout, elongated north—south direction.
5112	Gal. 12.6p; 10 in. RFL F/5.5 w/16mmKo. Very obvious, patch of light with a greater brighter middle, north—south orientation. Faint star close to southern edge. A bright star is nearby.
5128	Gal. 7.2p; 10 in. RFL F/5.5 w/16mmKo. Very bright, large, round object, cut through the middle by a wide dark lane. This galaxy was seen through a pair of 7 x 35 binoculars.
5139	Gb.Cl. 3.7v; 10 in. RFL F/5.5 w/16mmKo. *Very impressive*, this object far surpasses M13, larger with many more individual stars than M13, it has a definite 3-D effect which reminds me of a popcorn ball with many loose stars on its edges. This object is impressive regardless of the optical aid used. Seen with the naked eye as a faint but distinct patch of light.
5194 (M51)	Gal. 8.1v; 10 in. RFL F/5.5 w/16mmKo. Very large and bright galaxy, elliptical with a very large and bright condensed nucleus. The outer envelope is quite large and is mottled, with averted vision definite spiral structure is held steady. Two main arms are seen. In the southwest portion of the envelope there is a star that is rather obvious. I have seen this star easily in an 8 in. scope, while observations made some years ago with a 6 in. scope fail to mention it. The connecting arm, to 5195, cannot be seen. During moments of good seeing, the spiral structure was impressive indeed with the two main arms appearing fat and curved, and much

NGC 5194 Whirlpool Galaxy, NGC 5195 Companion Galaxy

NGC	DESCRIPTION
	brighter than the rest of the envelope. One exceptionally clear night while observing in Sonora, Mexico, spiral structure was repeatedly picked up (with averted vision) in M51, with a 6 in. F.8 scope! See 5195.
FIG. #5	NGC 5194 10 in. F/5.5 with 16mm ocular Notice star involved in the envelope, in the south—west region.
5195	Gal. 8.4v; 10 in. RFL F/5.5 w/16mmKo. Bright, roundish with a large envelope almost round except for a noticeably flattened portion on the side nearest to M51. The nucleus was bright, condensed and off center, easy.

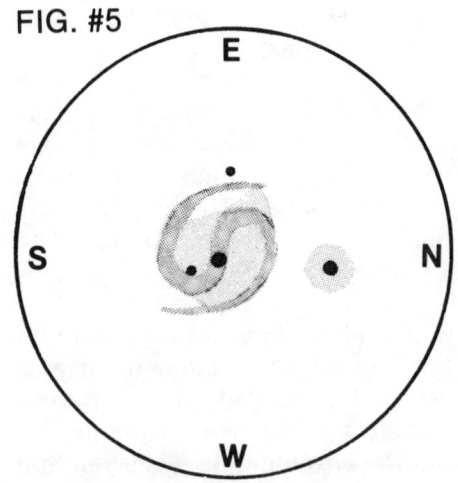

NGC	DESCRIPTION
5198	Gal. 12.9p; 10 in. RFL F/5.5 w/16mmKo. South on M51 but in the same field. Small, bright, patchlike, even brightness throughout, can be found while sweeping.
5236 (M83)	Gal. 10.1v; 6 in. RFL F/8 w/25mmO. Bright, roundish, very condensed brighter core, very large and diffuse outer envelope. Center may be stellar. Easy.

10 in. F/5.5 with 10.2mm ocular. Large and bright with a much brighter, very condensed core, but not quite stellar. It appears generally slightly elliptical, with two definitely brighter extensions going outward from the nucleus; one in the north—west direction and one in the south—east direction. These brighter "arms" are involved in a much larger, fainter, diffuse elliptical shaped outer envelope. Definite mottling seen throughout this larger diffuse envelope. With averted vision, I first noticed that the tips of the two brighter arms are curved slightly. This gives the galaxy a somewhat short "S" appearance. *Impressive!* The two brighter arms are very apparent with a 25mm ocular. There are two faint stars just beyond the tip of each brighter arm, one star near each tip. See Fig. #6.

FIG. #6

NGC 5236

10 in. F/5.5 with 10.2mm ocular

Drawing not to scale. Notice slight "S" shape of this galaxy. Impressive!

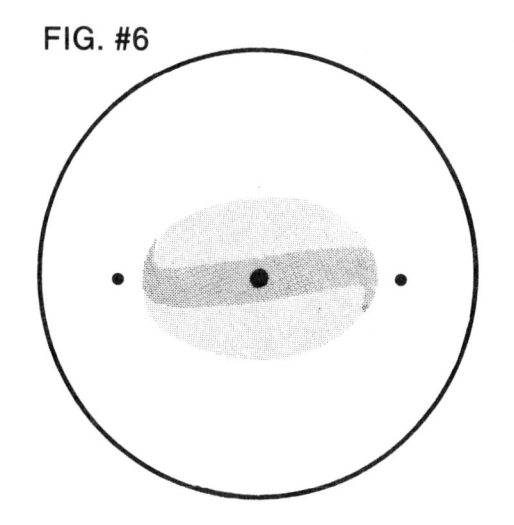

5253	Gal. 10.8p; 10 in. RFL F/6 w/31mmK. Bright, elongated with a small brighter core, averted vision extends the arms quite a bit.
5272 (M3)	Gb.Cl. 6.4v; 10 in. RFL F/6 w/10.5mmO. Exceptionally large and bright, condensed core with individual stars from the core area outwards. "Arms" seen to start near the core and flow outwards, *Impressive!*
5286	Gb.Cl. 8.5 mag; 10 in. F/5.5 w/16mmKo. Large, bright and easy to see. At first, it appears to have an even texture but averted vision shows a few individual stars on the outer edge.
5301	Gal. 13.p mag; 10 in. F/5.5 w/16mmKo. A small but distinct fuzzy object, can be found while sweeping.
5377	Gal. 11.2v mag; 10 in. F/5.5 w/16mmKo. Small, elongated, fuzzy

NGC	DESCRIPTION
	patch of light. Slight brightening near the center, much brighter than 5301, easily seen.
5422	Gal. 11.5v mag; 8 in. F/5 w/16mmKo. Smaller than expected but bright, elliptical, even brightness throughout, fuzzy patch of light, easy.
5448	Gal. 12.1p mag; 10 in. F/5.5 w/16mmKo. Easily seen while sweeping, medium sized, elongated east—west, a slightly brighter middle. Seen in a 6 in. F/8 scope.
5457 (M101)	Gal. 9.6v mag; 10 in. F/6 w/31mmK. *Very large* and bright, with a round, large, conspicuous outer envelope. A much brighter, off center core was seen. Averted vision showed some spiral structure in the envelope.
5473	Gal. 11.4v; 8 in. RFL F/5 w/16mmKo. Slightly fainter and slightly smaller than NGC 5822. Easily seen near a small chain of stars, this galaxy forming the fourth "star" in this chain.
5474	Gal. 11.4v mag; 8 in. F/5 w/16mmKo. Slightly elliptical, not very bright or large, definite mottled appearance, no sharp edges, with averted vision it appears slightly brighter in the northern postion.
5480	Gal. 12.6p mag; 10 in. F/5.5 w/16mmKo. Seen close to 5481. Of the two the galaxy to the north—west is 5480. It has a greater brighter middle, is round and smaller than 5448. It looks like a faint globular cluster. Seen in 6 in. scope.
5481	Gal. 13.5p mag; 10 in. F/5.5 w/16mmKo. Round with a greater brighter middle, looks like a faint globular cluster. Close to 5480, also seen in 6 in. scope but looked starlike.
5533	Gal. 12.6p mag; 10 in. F/5.5 w/16mmKo. Faint, small patch of light, slightly brighter towards the center.
5557	Gal. 11.6v mag; 10 in. F/5.5 w/16mmKo. Very much extended. Larger than 5533 or 5614 but fainter than both, even brightness throughout.
5566	Gal. 10.7v mag; 6 in. F/8 w/25mmO. Small, looks like a globular cluster, slightly brighter towards the center.
5576	Gal. 11.7v mag; 6 in. F/8 w/25mmO. Outside the field from 5566 but smaller and fainter than 5566. Appears at first like a fuzzy star, averted vision shows the outer envelope.
5614	Gal. 12.6p mag; 10 in. F/5.5 w/16mmKo. Appears to be the same size as 5533 but slightly brighter, round with a gradually brighter middle.
5660	Gal. 12.3p mag; 10 in. F/5.5 w/16mmKo. Fainter than 5676 which is in the same field. Patch appearance, no core seen. Seen in an 8 in. scope.

NGC	DESCRIPTION
5676	Gal. 11.2v mag; 10 in. F/5.5 w/16mmKo. Brighter than 5660, see preceding page. Slightly larger than 5660, a much brighter middle, faint extensions seen with averted vision, easy. Seen in an 8 in. scope.
5689	Gal. 11.4v mag; 10 in. F/5.5 w/16mmKo. Small patchlike with a bright core, extended diffuse envelope. Fainter than 5676 but slightly brighter than 5660.
5693	Gal. 14.5p mag; 10 in. F/5.5 w/16mmKo. Not listed in Skalnate Pleso Atlas. *Very* faint patch of light, but held steady without averted vision, may be elliptical. In the same field but south—southeast of 5689.
5694	Gb.Cl. 10.9p mag; 6 in. F/8 w/25mmO. Very small, appeared as a small patchlike object, accompanied by two obvious stars.
5740	Gal. 11.7v mag; 10 in. RFL F/6 w/16mmKo. Much smaller and fainter than NGC 5746, elliptical, even brightness throughout. Seen in 6 in. scope with averted vision.
5746	Gal. 10.1v mag; 6 in. F/8 w/25mmO. Edge on, thicker center with a slightly brighter core, sharp edges, easy.
5866 (M102)	Gal. 10.8v mag; 6 in. RFL F/8 w/25mmO. Elliptical, greater brighter middle, appears slightly north of two stars on either side of the galaxy, easy. Much brighter and smaller than NGC 5907.
5882	Pl.Nb. 10.5 neb; 10 in. F/5.5 w/16mmKo. Small but bright blue disk. 10.2mmO—Even brightness throughout, reminds me of NGC 3242 in Hydra.
5885	Gal. 12.4p mag; 10 in. RFL F/5.5 w/16mmKo. Bright patch of light, elliptical, bright star on outer edge, no bright core. Reminds me of the Merope nebula.
5897	Gb.Cl. 10.9v mag; 10 in. RFL F/5.5 w/16mmKo. Large and round with a few individual stars but the cluster is not resolved. Individual stars are seen at the edge of this cluster.
5904 (M5)	Gb.Cl. 6.2v mag; 6 in. RFL F/8 w/25mmO. Large and bright with a brighter center, individual stars seen about 2/3 of the way from the core area outward. Easy. Seen in 10 x 35 wide angle binoculars as a fuzzy patch.
5907	Gal. 11.3v mag; 6 in. RFL F/8 w/25mmO. Edge on, very long and thin, slightly thicker and slightly brighter core area. Easy and impressive.
5982	Gal. 10.9v mag; 10 in. RFL F/5.5 w/16mmKo. Smaller than 5985 but with a much brighter middle, round envelope. Close to 5985. Seen in a 6 in. F/8 but averted vision helped on the outer envelope (with a 25mm ocular).
5985	Gal. 11.4v mag; 10 in. RFL F/5.5 w/16mmKo. In the same field as

Region of Antares NGC 6121 (M4) Galaxy Cluster in lower right

NGC	DESCRIPTION
	5982 but larger than 5982 (almost four times larger). It has a granular appearance similar to NGC 6822. The slightly brighter core is off-center. The galaxy is elliptical shaped (very much extended) with no sharp edges. Seen in a 6 in. F/8 scope.
5986	Gb.Cl. 8.7v mag; 8 in. RFL F/5 w/16mmKo. Fairly bright globular, with some individual stars seen across the face of the cluster. Three stars seem to be the most obvious of these individual stars, giving this cluster a definite 3-D effect. Two of these obvious stars are seen to the right of center, one being red in color. One definite and one suspected star are seen to the left of center. All of these stars are on a straight line. This globular was seen in the 10 x 40mm finderscope. Impressive.
6015	Gal. 11.7p mag; 10 in RFL F/5.5 w/16mmKo. Similar in size to 5985, patch with even brightness, elongated north—south, easily found while sweeping. Seen in a 6 in. F/8 scope.
6052	Gal. 12.0p mag; 8 in. RFL F/5 w/16mmKo. Small, irregular shaped, faint patch of light. This galaxy is a little north of the position shown in the Skalnate Pleso Atlas. The two brighter stars (close to each other) shown in the Atlas, were in the same field as 6052.
6072	Pl.Nb. 14.1 neb/17.5 star; 10 in. RFL F/5.5 w/24mmKo. Faint, somewhat elliptical patch, green with a sharp edge. 12mmKo—A darker center is suspected with averted vision. 8mmKo—No

NGC	DESCRIPTION
	central star, darker center not seen. This planetary appears (visually) somewhat brighter than its listed magnitude (nebula) would have you expect. Seen in an 8 in. F/5 scope with a 16mm ocular.
6093 (M80)	Gb.Cl. 7.7v mag; 8 in. RFL F/5 w/32mmP. Very bright and very large, although smaller than M13. A very large and fuzzy outer shell with a distinctly brighter compact core. With this low power ocular, no mottling can be seen.
6118	Gal. 12.3p mag; 10 in. RFL F/5.5 w/25mmO. Very much extended patchlike appearance, faint with no sharp edges, averted vision not needed.
6121 (M4)	Gb.Cl. 6.4v mag; 8 in. RFL F/5 w/32mmP. Brighter and larger than M80. This globular looks a little elongated in the north—south direction, much brighter core. Individual stars in a tight group seem to cover the face of this globular, giving this cluster a 3-D effect. With this low power ocular, the outer envelope appears somewhat nebulous.
6124	Cl. 6.3v mag; 10 in. RFL F/5.5 w/24mmKo. Fills about 1/2 of the field including the outliers (stars), at least 60 stars total. The main portion of this cluster fills about 1/3 of the field. Seen in 7 x 35 binoculars as a large, fuzzy patch of light.
6139	Gb.Cl. 9.8p mag; 10 in. RFL F/5.5 w/24mmKo. Bright with a condensed core and a round fainter outer envelope, which is thin. The globular appears very condensed.
6153	Pl.Nb. 11.5 neb/-star; 10 in. RFL F/5.5 w/16mmKo. Just east of the cluster NGC 6124, appearing under low powers, as one of four stars in a trapezium of stars, obvious but has a small disk, sharp edge, no central star. 12mmKo—Round, green, does not appear uniformly bright with averted vision but may have a slightly darker center. Also seen in a 6 in. F/5 w/28mmKo as stellar, with 16mmKo a small but apparent disk was seen, knowing where to look.
6171 (M107)	Gb.Cl. 9.2v mag; 8 in. RFL F/5 w/32mmP. Round, uniform in brightness except for slight brightening towards the center, no individual stars seen, easy.
6181	Gal. 11.9v mag; 8 in. RFL F/5 w/16mmKo. Small, faint elliptical patch of light, even brightness throughout, no core smaller but brighter than NGC 6239.
6205 (M13)	Gb.Cl. 5.7v mag; 8 in. Celestron F/10 w/12mmK. Quite bright and large, fills most of the eyepiece, bright stars are seen as individuals and give it somewhat of a 3-D effect. Five individual outliers or curvilinear streams of stars are seen to travel from the center on outward. These outliers are very impressive. This globular rates second to Omega Centauri.
6207	Gal. 11.3v mag; 10 in. RFL F/5.5 w/16mmKo. Easily seen in the

NGC 6205 (M13) center, NGC 6207 Galaxy lower right

NGC	DESCRIPTION
	same field as M13 but on opposite ends of the field. Very elongated patch appearance, thicker at the center. Also seen in a 6 in. F/8 scope.
6210	Pl.Nb. 9.7 neb/12.5 star; 8 in. RFL F/5 w/16mmKo. Pale blue, bright with a small disk, easy. With a 25mm ocular the planetary appears nearly stellar. Seen in a 6 in. F/8 scope.
6218 (M12)	Gb.Cl. 6.6v mag; 6 in. RFL F/8 w/25mmO. Somewhat larger but a little fainter than M10. Individual stars seen except in the core. Less compact than M10. Seen in 10 x 35 wide-angle binoculars.
6229	Gb.Cl. 8.7v mag; 8 in. RFL F/5 w/25mmO. Bright and round, no individual stars seen, small in size. 10.2mmO—No individual stars seen.

NGC	DESCRIPTION
6239	Gal. 12.9p mag; 10 in. RFL F/5.5 w/24mmKo. Patchlike but seen with direct vision, no bright core, elongated approximately; north—south. Seen in a 6 in. F/5 with averted vision.
6254 (M10)	Gb.Cl. 6.7v mag; 8 in. RFL F/5 w/16mmKo. Large, bright, definite mottled appearance, brighter fuzzy core (not resolved), one obvious single star just outside nucleus.
6266 (M62)	Gb.Cl. 6.6v mag; 8 in. RFL F/5 w/32mmP. Very bright, brighter core area, round, no individual stars seen but some mottling is apparent.
6273 (M19)	Gb.Cl. 6.6v mag; 6 in. RFL F/8 w/25mmO. Brighter and larger than M9, slightly elongated, brighter core, mottling apparent in the outer edges.
6284	Gb.Cl. 9.7v mag; 6 in. RFL F/8 w/25mmO. Smaller than 6293, small bright core, round, general nebulous appearance, no individual stars seen.
6287	Gb.Cl. 9.9v mag; 10 in. RFL F/6.1 w/16mmKo. Brighter than 6342 and appears similar in size to 6356. Irregularly round with an even texture and brightness, no brighter core, no individual stars. Averted vision shows a hint of a slightly brighter core.
6293	Gb.Cl. 8.4v mag; 6 in. RFL F/8 w/25mmO. Fainter than 6356, round with a brighter core, smaller than M9. No individual stars seen.
6309	Pl.Nb. 11.6 neb/14.1 star; 10 in. RFL F/5.5 w/16mmKo. Close to a star of similar brightness, giving it a double star appearance. Gray-green, even brightness throughout, definitely elongated almost rectangular. I call this one the "Box Nebula." Seen in a 6 in. F/5 scope.
6333 (M9)	Gb.Cl. 7.3v mag; 10 in. RFL F/5.5 w/16mmKo. Very bright and large with a very compact core. Individual stars are scattered throughout. It appears as if this cluster is surrounded by a circle of stars. Generally the cluster stars fade gradually away from the center in an even sequence, except for the eastern edge which appeared flattened somewhat. The fading of the stars, gradually from the center outward, did not hold true for this eastern edge. On this edge, the stars stopped suddenly as if obscured by a dark nebula.
6341 (M92)	Gb.Cl. 6.1v mag; 6 in. RFL F/8 w/16mmKo. Bright, but a little smaller than M13, not exactly round, individual stars seen from the outer edges inwards but not into the core. 10.2mmKO— Cluster elongated somewhat north—south. Seen in the 10 x 40mm finderscope.
6342	Gb.Cl. 10.0v mag; 10 in. RFL F/6.1 w/16mmKo. Very small, smaller than M9 or NGC 6356. Small compact brighter core with a thin outer envelope, no individual stars seen. This globular is close to a star. Seen in a 6 in. F/8 scope.
6356	Gb.Cl. 8.7 mag; 10 in. RFL F/6.1 w/16mmKo. Smaller and fainter

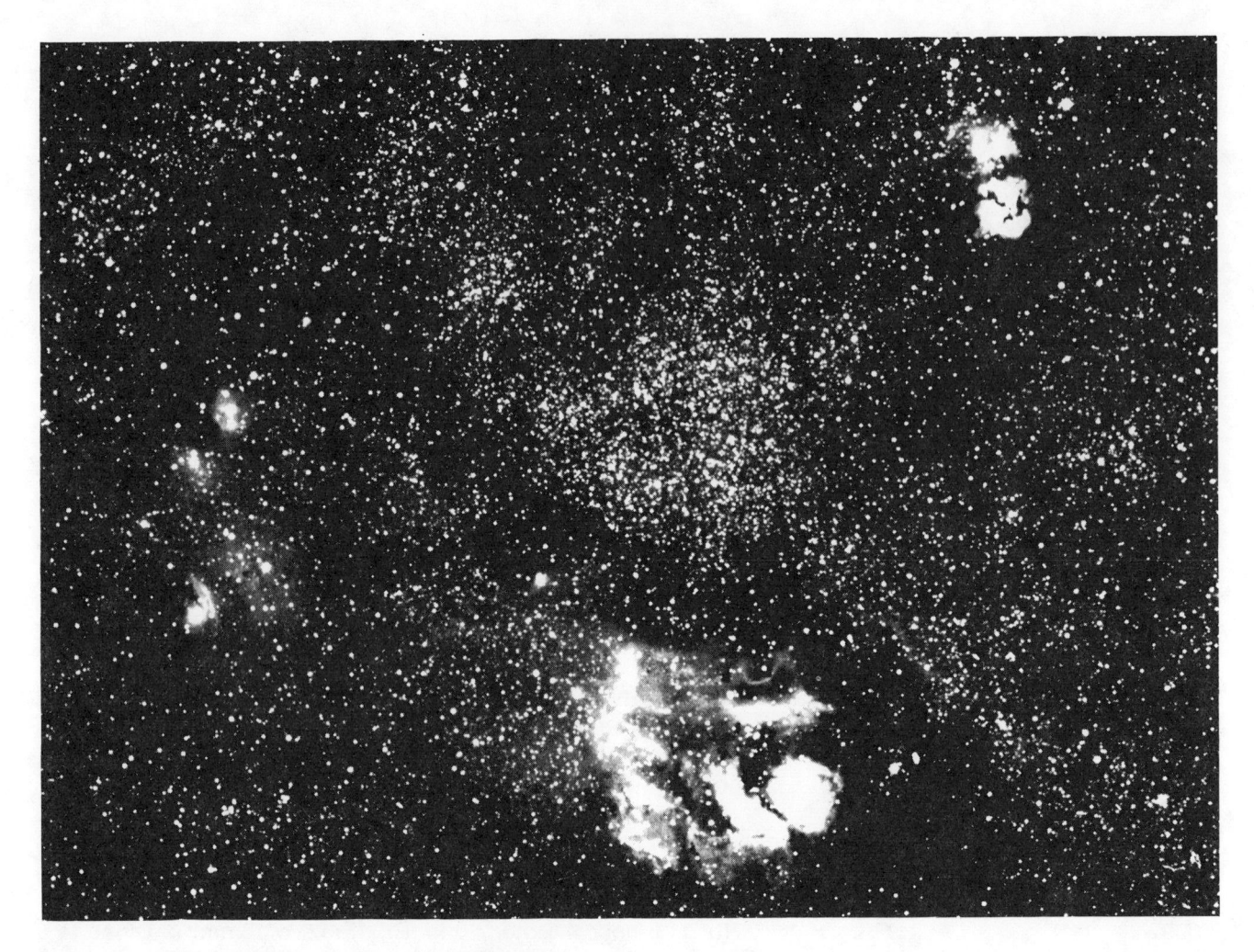

NGC 6514 (M20) Bright Nebula, NGC 6523 (M8)

NGC	DESCRIPTION
	than M9 but still fairly large and bright. It has a compact core that is brighter than the rest of the cluster. The stars gradually fade away from the core. No individual stars were seen but the edge does give the impression of graininess. Also seen in 6 in. F/8 scope.
6369	Pl.Nb. 9.9 neb/16.6 star, 28 sec of arc; 10 in. RFL F/6.1 w/16mmKo. Definite obvious disk with a darker center. Fainter than 6572 but somewhat larger. Round shape with a hint of a brighter condensed area in the northern part of the "Ring." 8mm—Confirms this brighter condensed region, it is seen with averted vision and "comes and goes" with the seeing conditions. It is as if there is a star involved with this portion of the ring.
6404 (M14)	Gb.Cl. 7.7 mag; 6 in. RFL F/8 w/25mmO. Very bright cluster with many individual stars. A small fuzzy core is seen.
6405 (M6)	Op.Cl. 5.3 mag; 7 x 50 binoculars. Smaller than M7, loose and more spread out. Bright and easy to find.
6440	Gb.Cl. 10.4 mag; 10 in. RFL F/5.5 w/25mmO. Very easy, fuzzy

NGC	DESCRIPTION
	patch with a brighter condensed core. No mottling seen with oculars ranging from 25mm to 6.8mm. Also seen in a 6 in. F/5 scope, both 6440 and 6445 were in same field in 6 in.
6441	Gb.Cl. 8.4 mag; 6 in. RFL F/8 w/25mmO. Fairly dim, round, fuzzy object, even brightness throughout. No bright core seen.
6444	Op.Cl.; 8 in. RFL F/5 w/16mmKo (not listed in Skalnate Pleso). Small, sparse, dim stars, irregular shape but not at all difficult. In the same field as NGC 6453.
6445	Pl.Nb. 13.2 neb/19.1 star, 38 x 29 sec of arc; 10 in. RFL F/5.5 w/16mmKo. Elongated disk with a definite dark center, faint and close to a star. The disk appears to be cut in half by the dark lane. Also seen with the 25mm ocular.
6453	Gb.Cl. 11.2p mag; 8 in. RFL F/5 w/16mmKo. Small, round, fuzzy patch, easily seen.
6475 (M7)	Op.Cl.; 8 in. RFL F/5 w/25mmO. Bright stars, fairly open or loose, scattered throughout and beyond the field. Seen with the naked eye as a bright patch of light.
6494 (M23)	Op.Cl. 6.9 mag; 6 in. RFL F/8 w/25mmO. Bright, large cluster fills the field of view.
6496	Gb.Cl. 9.7p mag; 6 in. RFL F/8 w/25mmO. Very faint, round, even brightness throughout.
6503	Gal. 9.6 mag; 8 in. RFL F/5 w/16mmKo. Bright, thick edge-on galaxy, thicker at the center with slight brightening at the center, no sharp edges.
6514 (M20)	B.N.; 8 in. RFL F/5 w/32mmP. Very large, very bright, western portion is the brightest. Dark lanes seen throughout with averted vision. Bright stars involved with nebulosity.
6520	Op.Cl. 8.1v mag; 8 in. Celestron, 16mmKo, 5 min. of arc. Small, round, two major bright stars involved. Seen as *eyes*, about 12 stars seen. Cluster is small but not concentrated.
6523 (M8)	B.N.; 8 in. RFL F/7 w/25mmO. Irregular shaped nebulosity with dark areas, just west of NGC 6530. Nebula appears to be touching western edge of 6530 and the nebulosity is very bright.
6530	Op.Cl. 6.3 mag; 8 in. RFL F/7 w/25mmO. Cluster made up of stars of similar magnitude, irregular shape, compact cluster.
6531 (M21)	Op.Cl. 6.5 mag; 6 in. RFL F/8 w/25mmO. Small, round cluster seen near nebula M20.
6541	Gb.Cl. 5.8 mag; 6 in. RFL F/8 w/25mmO. Bright with a much brighter core, round, no individual stars seen but a possible granular appearance detected at the edge.

Eagle Nebula NGC 6611 (M16)

NGC	DESCRIPTION
6543	Pl.Nb. 8.8 mag; 8 in. RFL F/5 w/16mmKo. Rather bright, but not too large, blue-green color, round disk, easy.
6563	Pl.Nb. 13.8 mag; 8 in. RFL F/5 w/16mmKo. Faint but obvious, round, pale gray color, forms a right triangle with two stars to the south.
6572	Pl.Nb. 9.6 mag; 10 in. RFL F/6.1 w/16mmKo. Seen as a very bright but small disk, even brightness throughout, no central star was seen. It has a green color with a definite hint of blue. 8mm shows it as being not perfectly round. With a 25mm ocular, the planetary could be mistaken for a star.
6574	Gal. 12.7 mag; 8 in. RFL F/5 w/16mmKo, 25mmO. 25mm shows it as stellar. 16mm—Very small, faint, irregular shaped patch of light with even brightness throughout.
6611 (M16)	Op.Cl. 6.4 mag; 10 x 35 binoculars. Seen as a round fuzzy patch, smaller and dimmer than M22.
6613 (M18)	Cl.; 6 in. RFL F/8 w/25mm. Seen as a small cluster of about 25 stars which spread outward from a small center.

NGC	DESCRIPTION
6618 (M17)	B.N.; 6 in. RFL F/8 w/25mmO. Very bright, extended object almost looks like a galaxy. Seen in 10 x 35 binoculars as was M18.
6626 (M28)	Gb.Cl. 7.3 mag; 6 in. RFL F/8 w/25mmO. Small, with a bright center, outer shell not seen. Using an 8 in. F/5 with a 32mm ocular, the thin outer shell was seen.
6629	Pl.Nb. 10.6 mag; 6 in. RFL F/8 w/25mmO. Very small, faint, patch like, no definite shape but a possible brighter center was seen with averted vision.
6637 (M69)	Gb.Cl. 8.9 mag; 8 in. RFL F/5 w/32mmP. Slightly larger than M70, a brighter core is seen with an outer shell that is greater than that of M70, easy.
6643	Gal. 11.3 mag; 8 in. RFL F/5 w/16mmKo. Average size and brightness, diffuse with no sharp edges, shape uncertain, even brightness throughout almost touching two faint but equal (brightness) stars.
6656 (M22)	Gb.Cl. 5.9 mag; 6 in. RFL F/8 w/25mmO. Much brighter, large core with a large outer envelope. Stars appear to begin to resolve at the outer edge.
6681 (M70)	Gb.Cl. 9.6 mag; 8 in. RFL F/5.5 w/32mmP. Similar to M54 but a little smaller and a fainter core. Round outer envelope, easy.
6694 (M26)	Op.Cl. 9.3 mag; 6 in. RFL F/8 w/25mmO. Seen as a tightly packed group of individual stars, round in shape. A dark band was seen entering the cluster from the west.
6705 (M11)	Op.Cl. 6.3 mag; 6 in. RFL F/8 w/25mmO, 9mm—(25mm). Small, compact and bright. Two dark areas penetrate from the south. Bright reddish star near the apex. Stars are of about similar magnitude with a fairly even distribution. (9mm)—Almost fills the field, darker areas prominent.
6712	Gb.Cl. 8.9 mag; 8 in. RFL F/5 w/25mmO. Small unresolved cluster, fuzzy greater brighter middle, same field as IC1295, easy.
6715 (M54)	Gb.Cl. 7.1 (photo) mag; 8 in. RFL F/5 w/32mmP. Smaller than M22 but brighter than M28. Very bright core but it is smaller than the core of M28, easy.
6720 (M57)	Pl.Nb. 9.3 neb/14.7 star; 10 in. RFL F/5.5 w/12mmKo. Very large and bright, annular, very thick donut, small star just outside ring seen with direct vision. A strong impression given that the dark center has a possible brighter spot or area in it. This effect was seen only with the 12mm ocular on this particular night. This effect is not usually seen with this telescope. High and low power oculars were used, but a "brighter spot" was not seen. Note: Since this observation was made, *numerous* others have also been made, with the end result of not having seen a "brighter spot."

NGC 6656 (M22)

NGC 6705 (M11) Cluster and Star clouds

NGC	DESCRIPTION
6723	Gb.Cl. 6.0 (photo) mag; 6 in. RFL F/8 w/25mmO. Medium sized round, steadily brightening from the outer edge to the center, quite diffuse.
6741	Pl.Nb. 11.7 neb/16.7 star; 16 in Cass. F/11 w/12mmK. Not quite round but slightly elongated, gray color with a hint of silver, slight brightening in the middle, diffuse but bright, very obvious. Seen in 10 in. F/5 w/12mm.
6751	Pl.Nb. 12.2 neb/13.3 star; 10 in. RFL F/5.5 w/16mmKo. Small green disk, even brightness throughout, no central star or darker area seen, obvious. 25mm—This planetary could be missed because of its small size. Seen in a 6 in. F/5 with a 16mm ocular, it looked stellar in appearance.
6760	Gb.Cl. 10.7 mag; 10 in. RFL F/5.5 w/12mmKo. Round, even textured, no mottling.
6779 (M56)	Gb.Cl. 8.2 mag; 6 in. RFL F/8 w/25mmO. Round, dim, fuzzy core, individual stars glimpsed on outer edge.
6781	Pl.Nb. 12.5 neb/15.4 star; 6 in. RFL F/5 w/16mmKo. Round, obvious disk, diffuse, large and easy. No bright core and appears fainter on northern edge.
6804	Pl.Nb. 13.3 neb/13.3 star; 10 in. RFL F/5.5 w/24mmKo. Appears somewhat fan shaped, diffuse, no central star or darker center. Northern edge very close to an obvious star. Seen in an 8 in. RFL F/5 with a 16mm ocular.
6809 (M55)	Gb.Cl. 4.4 (photo) mag; 7 x 50 binoculars. Seen as a dim, round, fuzzy object, but not difficult to see. No individual stars seen.
6818	Pl.Nb. 9.9 neb/15.0 star; 10 in. RFL F/5.5 w/16mmKo. Not perfectly round but definite flattening at the poles, bright blue color, even brightness throughout, very easy. Seen with a 6 in. F/8 scope with a 25mm ocular.
6822	Gal. 9.2 (photo) mag; 8 in. RFL F/5 w/16mmKo. Large, dim, definite patch of light granular in texture, covers about 1/4 of the field. At least six foreground stars seen involved with the galaxy. A hard galaxy for the amateur to find as its light is spread out over a large area and looks like a brightening of the background field. NGC 6818 is just outside the field.
6826	Pl.Nb. 8.8 neb/10.8 star; 8 in. RFL F/5 w/10.2mmO. Easily seen as a bright, blue-white disk. Central star is prominent with the blinking effect noticeable with averted vision. Also seen with a 3-1/2 in. Questar although the blinking effect was not apparent.
6838 (M71)	Gb.Cl. 9.0 mag; 8 in. RFL F/5 w/32mmP. It looks like a very compact open cluster, nebulous with a grayish center. Very "soft" appearance.
6853 (M27)	Pl.Nb. 7.6 neb/13.4 star; 8 in. RFL F/5 w/6.8mmO. Very large,

Ring Nebula Lyra NGC 6720 (M57)

Dumbell Nebula NGC 6853 (M27)

NGC	DESCRIPTION
	almost rectangular shaped with turned edges, diffuse, center of the nebula very bright with a darker area or two opposing protrusions giving it a "bow-tie" appearance. Seen in 6 x 40 finderscope as a patch of light.
6864 (M75)	Gb.Cl. 8.0 mag; 8 in. RFL F/5 w/32mmP. Very small, round, with a small bright core. Appears as a fuzzy star.
6894	Pl.Nb. 14.4 neb/17.0 star; 10 in. RFL F/6 w/16.3mmG. Obvious, easily seen as a medium sized disk with a sharp outer edge. A possible darker center seen with averted vision. Seen with an 8 in. F/5 scope.
6913 (M29)	Op.Cl. 7.1 mag; 6 in. RFL F/8 w/40mm. Very small, compact open star cluster. It has somewhat of a box shape with one star protruding. Located in an area with many background stars.
6939	Op.Cl. 10.0 mag; 8 in. RFL F/5 w/16mmKo. Same field as NGC 6946. Large, compact, irregular shaped cluster, stars are faint. Faint nebulous glow (unresolved stars) seen near center of cluster.
6946	Gal. 9.7 (photo) mag; 8 in. RFL F/5 w/16mmKo. Large, face on with slight brightening towards the center, patch appearance with a few scattered stars. Seen in a 3-1/2 in. Questar scope.
6960	Bt.Nb.; 8 in. RFL F/5 w/16mmKo. Fills the field of view. Star 52 Cygni involved with nebulosity, which is a very long, thin nebula. Northern extension is brighter, more sharply defined and is "bent." Southern extension is fainter and less sharply defined as it just continues to fade away.
6974	Bt.Nb.; 8 in. RFL F/5 w/16mmKo. Possibly seen with averted vision as a slightly brighter patch found between the two brighter portions of the Veil Nebula (NGC 6960 and 6992).
6981 (M72)	Gb.Cl. 9.8 mag; 6 in. RFL F/8 w/25mmO. Just west of M73, but outside the field. Small, round cluster, slight brightening in the center.
6992	Bt.Nb.; 10 in. RFL F/5.5 w/24mmKo. Much more obvious than NGC 6960, as seen in the same scope. Definite sharp edges, slight mottling apparent with averted vision, nebula curves and goes beyond the field. The southern portion of the nebula fans out and is very obvious.
6994 (M73)	Group of stars; 6 in. RFL F/8 w/25mmO. At first glance it looked like three stars in a compact group, having a definite fuzzy appearance. Closer inspection shows four stars total, all about the same brightness, in a very compact group.
6995	Cluster in 6992; 8 in. RFL F/5 w/16mmKo. A group of bright stars at the southern tip (fan shaped tip) of NGC 6992. These stars are conspicuous and are involved with the nebulosity NGC 6992.

Veil Nebula NGC 6960

NGC 7078 (M15)

NGC	DESCRIPTION
7000	Bt.Nb. Naked Eye. Seen as a definite brighter portion of the Milky Way, irregular shape close to the area near the Gulf of Mexico.
7008	Pl.Nb. 13.3 neb/12.9 star; 6 in. RFL F/8 w/25mmO. Larger than average, pale, touching a brighter star, has patch appearance, even brightness throughout.
7009	Pl.Nb. 8.4 neb/11.7 star; 6 in. RFL F/8 w/25mmO. Disk appearance, green-blue color, easy. Poles appear slightly compressed with an 8 in. Celestron and a 25mm ocular.
7078 (M15)	Gb.Cl. 6.0v mag; 10 in. RFL F/5.5 w/10.2mmO. Very bright, condensed much brighter core (off center). Five separate stragglers (arms) of individual stars seen to radiate outwards from the core. No darker area was seen in or about the core area. Quick fading of stars was noticed from the core outwards.
7089 (M2)	Gb.Cl. 6.3v mag; 8 in. Celestron w/40mmK, 25mmK, 12mmK, 40mmK. Very large, bright, individual stars seen from the outer edge inwards, very bright center. 25mmK—Individual stars are seen closer to the center. 12mmK—A few stars are seen close to the center. This is indeed a beautiful globular cluster!
7092 (M39)	Op.Cl. 5.2v mag; 6 in. F/8 w/40mmK. About ten bright stars in a field of view filled with stars. The cluster goes beyond the field of view. The many fainter background stars makes identification of cluster members uncertain. This cluster was seen in a pair of 7 x 50 binoculars as a small fuzzy patch of light with a few individual stars involved.
7099 (M30)	Gb.Cl. 8.4v mag; 2.4 in. RR F/12 w/20mmHy. Smaller and fainter than M2 as seen in the same scope. Brighter central core that is smaller and fainter than the core in M2. A mottled appearance is suspected. Cluster not seen in 5 x 24 finderscope.
7177	Gal. 12.0 (photo) mag; 6 in. RFL F/8 w/25mmO. Very small, smaller than NGC 7217, easily seen as a fuzzy roundish object, even brightness throughout.
7184	Gal. 12.0 (photo); 6 in. RFL F/8 w/25mmO. Very elongated, brighter than NGC 7723 fainter than NGC 7727, but longer than either one.
7217	Gal. 11.0 (photo) mag; 6 in. RFL F/8 w/25mmO. Larger than NGC 7332, elliptical shaped, brighter core, easy.
7293	Pl.Nb. 6.5 neb/13.3 star; 6 in. RFL F/8 w/25mmO. Seen in 6 x 30 finder and 10 x 35 wide angle binoculars. In telescope it was a very large patch, about 1/3 size of full moon. Round with dark patches throughout. Not more difficult to see than the Veil Nebula. Impressive!
7331	Gal. 9.7 mag; 10 in. RFL F/5.5 w/25mmO. Very obvious, bright, elongated object. 12mm—Very bright with a gradually brighter middle, north—south orientation, well-defined edge with a hint of a "straight-edge" on the western side. Seen in a 6 in. F/8 scope.

NGC	DESCRIPTION
FIG. #7	NGC 7331
	8 in. F/10 Schmidt-Cassegrain with 16mm ocular
	Larger galaxy, north—south extension, is NGC 7331. Small galaxy, east—west extension, is NGC 7335. Use averted vision on 7335, to locate.
7332	Gal. 11.8 mag; 6 in. RFL F/8 w/25mmO. Small, faint, almost starlike.
7448	Gal. 11.2 mag; 6 in. RFL F/8 w/25mmO. Faint, elongated patch of light, brighter than NGC 7479, even brightness throughout.
7457	Gal. 12.2 mag; 6 in. RFL F/8 w/25mmO. Faint, averted vision helps, slightly brighter core, elliptical shape. Appears similar in size to NGC 7217.
7479	Gal. 11.6 mag; 6 in. RFL F/8 w/25mmO. Elliptical shape, patch appearance, even brightness throughout, reminds me of M74.
7510	Op.Cl. 8.8 mag; 8 in. RFL F/5 w/10.2mmO. Both NGC 7635 and NGC 7510 are seen in the same field when using a 16mm ocular. 10.2mm—Appears very narrow, elongated, six stars being brighter than the rest.
7606	Gal. 11.5 mag; 6 in. RFL F/8 w/25mmO. Small fuzzy object, faint. 18mm—Elongated and easy to see, no brighter core seen.
7635	Pl.Nb. 8.5 neb/8.5 star; 8 in. RFL F/5 w/16mmKo. Two stars close together involved in nebula, roundish is shape, faint and large. 3-1/2 in. Questar w/40x—Knowing exactly where to look, the two stars seen in the 8 in. scope are identified as one star in slight nebulosity in the 3-1/2 scope.
7640	Gal. 11.3 (photo) mag; 8 in. RFL F/5 w/25mmO. Faint, slightly larger than average, edge on, wedged between three stars which all appear to be touching the galaxy with the exception of the star near the nucleus.
7645 (M52)	Op.Cl. 7.3v mag; 8 in. RFL F/5 w/16mmKo. Appears as a half circle of stars, with the brighter members forming a triangle. No background glow seen. 3-1/2 in. Questar with an ocular giving 40 power—Triangular shaped cluster with some background glow seen to one side of the triangle. 7 x 50 binoculars—Small fuzzy patch of light.

NGC	DESCRIPTION
7662	Pl.Nb. 8.9 neb/12.5 star; 16 in. Cass., F/11 w/24mm. Bright, large, round disk, blue-gray color, somewhat like a snowball with a fuzzy edge. A small dark core was glimpsed. 16mm—Dark core is easier to see though very small. This dark core is round but it is not a truly black area.
7678	Gal. 12.5 (photo) mag; 6 in. RFL F/8 w/25mmO. Very faint and required averted vision. The galaxy is situated between three faint stars.
7723	Gal. 11.1 mag; 6 in. RFL F/8 w/25mmO. Slightly smaller than NGC 7727 and dimmer. Shape may have been slightly elliptical.
7727	Gal. 10.7 mag; 6 in. RFL F/8 w/24mmO. Round, fuzzy patch of light.
7741	Gal. 11.6 (photo) mag; 6 in. RFL F/8 w/25mmO. Very faint smudge of light, use averted vision, touching a brighter star, hard.

B86 Dark Nebula

TELESCOPIC OBSERVATIONS OF NON-NGC OBJECTS INCLUDING: INDEX CATALOG (IC), DARK NEBULAE, MISCELLANEOUS

INDEX CATALOG

IC	DESCRIPTION
289	Pl.Nb. 12.3 neb/15.0 star; 45 x 30 sec of arc, Cass.; 10 in. RFL F/5.5 w/16, 12, 10mm. 16mm—Very small, green disk, faint. 12mm—Even brightness throughout, pale greenish color gives it a ghost type image. 10.2mm—Possibly slightly brighter towards the center.
342	Gal. 12.0 mag; 8 in. RFL F/5 w/16mmKo. Very small, round, faint fuzzy object. There is a faint outer glow surrounding a brighter starlike core. Could be missed for a star. Shown in Skalnate Pleso but not listed in the Atlas Coeli Catalog.
349	B.N., 30 x 30 min of arc, Taurus; 10 in. RFL F/5.5 w/25mm. Large and very obvious, balloon shaped, fills about 1/2 field of view. 8 in. RFL F/5 w/16mm—Very easy to see, large and fairly bright, bluish-white color, appears as a large oval with the star Merope near one edge. 6 in. RFL F/8 w/25mm—Averted vision not needed, fan shaped, large, almost fills the field of view, diffuse, bluish-white color.
351	Pl.Nb. 12.4 neb/15.0 star, 8 x 6 sec of arc, Perseus; 10 in. RFL F/5.5 w/16, 12, 16mm. Very small, slightly green color, fuzzy disk. 12mm—Confirms disk, appears to be even in brightness throughout. Two stars are seen around this planetary (also seen with 16mm). Of these two stars, the fainter one precedes the nebula, while the brighter star is just northeast of the planetary. Both stars are equidistant from the planetary. This planetary is at the apex of a triangle formed by the two stars and the planetary.
361	Op.Cl. 11.2 v, Camelopardalis; 8 in. RFL F/5 w/25, 16mm. 25mm—faint, fuzzy patch of light with a few individual stars seen in the glow. 16mm—Irregular patch, mottling seen in background glow

IC	DESCRIPTION
	with some individual stars.
410 (& NGC 1893)	B.N., 23 x 20 min of arc, Auriga; 10 in. RFL F/5.5 w/25, 16mm. This nebula is associated with the open star cluster NGC 1893. 16mm—About 1/4 field of view in size, large, shaped similar to an inverted "Y" with the two shorter arms widely separated. About six brighter stars form the main "Y" portion of the cluster (1893). Minor stars fill out this "Y" shaped cluster. IC410 is seen along the "Y" axis as a soft glow. Of the two short extensions, the westernmost one has a brighter glow than the rest of the "Y." This brighter portion of IC410 is enhanced when using averted vision. In the stem of the "Y," their are two bright stars, and at the end of each shorter arm (two of them), there is a bright star. No definite shape to IC410, but more or less bright patches sporadically against the "Y" shaped cluster. 25mm—IC410 is seen as a faint patch of light with very low contrast.
418	Pl.Nb. 12.0 neb/10.9 star, 14 x 11 sec of arc, Lepus; 10 in. RFL F/5.5 w/16mm. Small, very bright light blue, round fuzzy object, definite brightening towards the center.
434	B.N., 60 x 10 min of arc, 8 in. RFL F/5 w/16mmKo. Bright diffuse nebula seen with direct vision, traveling outward from Zeta Orionis south. Long, thin, cone shaped; base of cone situated towards Zeta Orionis. Edges of this nebula are rather diffuse. Just becuase this bright nebula is seen does not necessarily mean that the Horsehead Nebula (B33) will be seen. Use a low power wide field ocular when viewing IC434. See B33.
724	Gal. 13.8p, Not in Skalnate Pleso, Virgo; 10 in. RFL F/5.5 w/16mm. It is located just northwest of the star Xi Virgo, which can be found on the Skalnate Pleso Chart No. 8. It appeared as a faint possibly elliptical shaped object, patch appearance. Fainter than NGC 3976. (IC724—R.A. 11h 41m +9.13).
1287	B.N., 44 x 34 min of arc, Scutum; 10 in. RFL F/5.5 w/16mm. Surrounds a double star. Brighter star is white while the fainter companion is a blue-green color. These stars appear to be surrounded by a roundish, rather large haze. It looks similar to stars as seen through optics that have dewed up in the early morning hours. This haze is rather easy to see.
1295	Pl.Nb. 15v, 120 x 90 sec of arc, Scutum; 8 in. RFL F/5 w/25, 16mm. The Atlas Coeli lists the magnitude of this object as being 15th magnitude, while my own visual observations place this object as being closer to 13th magnitude. 25mm—Seen without averted vision as a patch of light slightly brighter than the background, irregular shaped, could easily be missed. 16mm—Larger than average sized, faint diffuse patch, definite edge, roundish with a dark center, generally appearing as a fat "U" shaped object. No bright core seen. A dark lane cuts through 3/4 of this object. The southern portion of this "U" is brighter and slightly larger than the northern portion. Not at all difficult to see. Interesting!

IC	DESCRIPTION
1470	Pl.Nb. 8.1 neb/11.9 star, 70 x 45 sec of arc, Cepheus, F/10 w/25, 16, 12mm. 25mm—Near a star of equal magnitude, small, faint, round envelope, bright central star, use averted vision to locate. 16mm—Obvious brighter center with a large round envelope, easy with direct vision. 12mm—Obvious starlike center with a slightly elliptical outer envelope. Star is off center towards the northern portion of the envelope.
1727	Gal. 12.2p, Triangulum; 10 in. RFL F/5.5 w/16mm. Very close to NGC 672. Much fainter and slightly smaller than NGC 672. Use averted vision to locate.
1747	Pl.Nb. 13.6 neb/15.0 star, 13 sec of arc; 16 in. Cass., F/11 w/24, 16mm. Small, faint, round disk, even brightness throughout, easy to miss. 16mm—With averted vision, a possible darkening in the center is suspected.
2003	Pl.Nb. 12.6 neb/18.4 star, 5 sec of arc, Perseus; 10 in. F/5.5 w/16, 12, 10.2mm. 16mm—*Very* small pale green disk. 12mm—Disk more apparent, disk has sharp edge, even brightness throughout, one star seen on western edge outside of disk. Nebula is seen with direct vision, and is contained within a scattered group of several obvious stars. 10.2mm—Disk very obvious, fairly easy to see. Outer edge of planetary is still sharp.
2149	Pl.Nb. 9.9 neb/14.0 star, 15 x 10 sec of arc, Auriga; 10 in. RFL F/5.5 w/25, 16, 10.2, 6.8mm. 25mm—Could easily be mistaken for a blue star. 16mm—Small fuzzy blue dot. 10.2mm—Brighter star at center suspected with averted vision. 6.8mm—Bright center not now apparent. Nebula does not have sharp borders, small oval in size.
2165	Pl.Nb. 12.5 neb/16.8 star, 9 x 7 sec of arc, Canis Major; 10 in. RFL F/5.5 w/32, 12, 10, 2mm. 12mm—First seen as a very small disk, blue-green in color and evenly bright. A diffraction grating was used to confirm this planetary nebula. 10.2mm—Disk still evenly bright (also used 6.8mm but no difference in brightness). 32mm—Appears as a rather obvious star, identified with the diffraction grating. Once this disk was seen (using 12mm), it was then apparent with the 16mm ocular.
2395	Op.Cl. 4.6v, 10 min of arc, 16 stars, Vela; 7 x 50 binoculars. Easily seen while sweeping. A large bright glow with about six individual stars scattered throughout. It looks like it belongs somewhere in the Sagittarius—Scorpio region, because of its brightness.
2627	Gal. 12.8p, 2.0 x 1.6, Crater; 10 in. RFL F/6 w/16mm. Very small, slightly brighter center, looks like a small globular cluster. Seen with direct vision. This galaxy was not seen in a 6 in. RFL F/8 using a 25mm ocular.
3568	Pl.Nb. 11.6 neb/12.0 star, 18 sec of arc, Camelopardalis; 8 in. RFL F/5 w/25, 16, 6.8mm. 16mm—Small, fuzzy round object looks like an out of focus star with a bright core. 6.8mm—Small, round,

IC	DESCRIPTION
	bright with a much brighter core. 25mm—Starlike. With my 6.8mm ocular it reminds me a little of NGC 40.
4406	Pl.Nb. 10.6n, 100 x 37 sec of arc, Lupus; 10 in. RFL F/5.5 w/16, 10.2mm. 16mm—Small, bright, disk shaped object. 10.2mm—Disk with sharp edges, even brightness throughout, no star or dark center seen.

8 in. RFL F/5 w/25, 10.2mm. 25mm—Appears starlike. 10.2mm—A fuzzy disk appearing out of focus, round, no sharp edge, pale green color, easily seen. |
| 4593 | Pl.Nb. 10.2 neb/10.2 star, 15 x 11 sec of arc, Hercules; 10 in. RFL F/5.5 w/10.2mm. Incorrectly listed as being in the constellation of Serpens Caput, in the Atlas Coeli Catalog. 10.2mm—Small, very slightly extended but looks more roundish, a white color with a hint of blue, fuzzy disk with no sharp edge. With averted vision a gradually brighter core is suspected. Using a 25mm ocular this planetary appeared stellar. |

FIG. #8

IC 4593

10 in. F/5/5 with 10.2mm ocular

The planetary nebula is marked with an arrow.

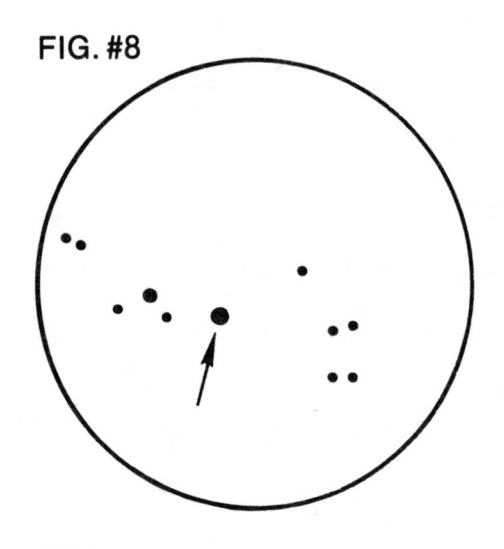

4634	Pl.Nb. 12.3 neb/17.4 star, 20 x 9 sec of arc, Ophiuchus; 10 in. RFL F/5.5 w/16mm. Appeared about the same size and color as IC4593. Small, slightly extended disk, white but with a more pronounced touch of blue, giving it a more whitish-blue color. Bright but small. This is the first planetary nebulae in which I tried the diffraction grating...Success! All of the brighter stars showed a small but obvious spectrum. The planetary, however, showed a duplicate image of itself, to either the right or left hand edge of the field. It appeared as another "extra" star or disk in the field.
4725 (M25)	Op.Cl. 6.5v mag; 6 in. RFL F/8 w/25mmO, 9mmO. 25mm—Very large open star cluster, fills the field of view with many bright stars, irregular shaped cluster. 9mm—The cluster effect is somewhat lost in this narrow field, as the bright stars are everywhere, going beyond the field. 7 x 50 binoculars—Small but bright cluster, a few individual stars seen. An easy object.
5146	B.N. 10.0s, 12 x 12 min of arc, Cygnus; 8 in RFL F/5 w/25mm. Smaller and dimmer than NGC 281. Shape may be unevenly

IC	DESCRIPTION
	round, somewhat of a baseball diamond with rounded corners. Two brighter stars, one on each end. Use averted vision to locate, then not needed. Diffuse patch of light was slightly brighter than the background sky but was still definite.

DARK NEBULAE

B	DESCRIPTION
33 (Horsehead)	8 in. RFL F/5 w/16mmKo. Seen with averted vision as a dark protrusion into the bright nebula IC434. The bright nebula, IC434, was easily seen with direct vision. B33 itself appeared as a small "cut" into IC434; it was somewhat bean shaped. Using a 20mm Erfle ocular, B33 was seen with averted vision, but was more difficult than with the 16mm ocular.
72	Ophiuchus; 10 in. RFL F/6.1 w/16mm. The star on the southern tip of the "S" nebula was found and placed near the bottom of the field. Immediately, I saw some non-uniform brighter patches of nebulosity. The darker "S" shaped nebula was not actually seen clearly, but the brighter nebulosity traced out a definite 1/2 of an "S," with this 1/2 "S" or "U" shaped object having the star (already mentioned) at its apex. This "U" shaped area was seen without difficulty.
86	Sagittarius; 8 in. Celestron w/16mm. Near NGC 6520. Very obvious and large, about three times the size of 6520. Clearly seen to the west of 6520. Irregularly oblong object, north—south orientation, three obvious stars involved. The background sky is slightly brighter than B86, two stars closest to 6520...northern one is the brighter. The third star is the westernmost and is the faintest of the three. A bright chain of stars, in a north—south direction, is seen just outside and to the west of B86.
92	Sagittarius; 8 in. Celestron w/16mm. Best contrast shown with 16mm ocular. Looks similar to photo's, slightly oblong with only one star seen which was off center. Background sky here contains many more dark areas than does the area around B86. This whole area is wonderful with a wide field ocular. There is a dark nebula east of B92 which is connected to B92 by a thin arm... Interesting!
142	Aquila; 10 in. RFL F/5.5 w/24mm. Thicker than B143, but just one large elongated dark patch, somewhat more obvious than B143, impressive. Seen with 7 x 35 binoculars!
143	Aquila; 10 in. RFL F/5.5 w/24mm. Very obvious, fills entire field. Dark nebula against a populated starry background...impressive! Southern arm more prominent and thicker than northern arm. Looks like a large, thick horseshoe, thickest at back end (curve) opposite opening. Knowing where to look, it was seen in 7 x 35 binoculars.

IC434, B33 Horsehead Nebula

MISCELLANEOUS OBSERVATIONS

DESCRIPTION

NEW 1
Gal. 12.8p, 3.5 x 3.5 min of arc, Cetus; 10 in. RFL F/5.5 w/16mm. Just outside the 16mm field and to the east of NGC 357. This galaxy (NEW 1) was harder to see but was slightly larger than NGC 357. It was round, gradually brighter towards the center and was seen with direct vision.

Mel 22 (M45) Pleiades
Op.Cl. 1.4v mag; 8 in. RFL F/8 w/25mmO. The entire field is filled with stars, some being very bright. The blue-white stars are not close together but rather are somewhat evenly spaced apart. Against a dark sky, these stars have a jewel-like quality that make this cluster an impressive sight through a telescope. With the naked eye, under excellent sky conditions, 12 stars were seen without much difficulty. For information regarding the Merope Nebula, see the IC349 observations.

(M24)
Star Cloud, 4.5 mag; 8 in. RFL F/8 w/25mmO. Entire field filled with stars, a few brighter ones. The field of this scope is too small to see the entire object. Rectangular shaped prominent with dark area (B92) noticeable near northern edge, about mid-region of star cloud. Star cluster NGC 6603 easily seen in northern portion of M24. 7 x 50 binoculars. See photo page 116.

Winnecke 4 (M40)
Double Star, 9.0 & 9.3 mag; 10 in. RFL F/5.5 w/24mmKo. Very obvious, widely separated double star, blue-white color (no nebulosity). The galaxy NGC 4290 is in the same field of view.

MISCELLANEOUS NOTES

NOTE REGARDING B33

I definitely do not want to give the reader the impression that the Horsehead nebula (B33) is an easy object to see. . . . it is not! Before achieving success, I had searched for this dark nebula on many occasions over a three year period without ever seeing it. I had accepted the fact that B33 was beyond the reach of telescopes 10 inches or smaller. On many of those unsuccessful nights I distinctly saw the long luminous band, IC 434, as a fairly easy object with direct vision.

When I wanted to look for B33, I would wait for a night of above average to excellent seeing. Then one night to my total surprise, B33 was seen while routinely looking for it. I had not expected to see it. On this particular night it was so obvious with averted vision, that I must have stared at it in disbelief for a good ten minutes. B33 was so conspicious that I was able to show it to another experienced deep-sky observer, who had no difficulty whatsoever in seeing it.

Throughout the observing session, at least a dozen times, I went back to B33 and confirmed what I had seen. When I looked up at the sky on this particular night, it did not appear noticeably different from other nights noted as well above average to excellent—but for some reason this night was different!

Over the years, after the B33 sighting, I have attempted to observe this object again using scopes in the 8-inch to 10-inch range for most of my viewing. Usually, B33 is not even suspected. So far, I have not been able to repeat that particular sighting of B33. . . but I keep trying. When those rare excellent nights arrive, the amateur can only hope that he is out there, observing through his telescope.

M24 NOTE

In the past, there has been some confusion as to the identity of the deep-sky object known as M24 because it was mistaken for another deep-sky object. Some references cite M24 as being a detached portion (star cloud) of the Milky Way in Sagittarius region, while others note it as being a small star cluster known as NGC 6603. To add to this confusion, the star cluster (NGC 6603) is located within the border of the Star Cloud mentioned above. Let's look at some statistics of these two objects. The Star Cloud has a magnitude of 4.6 and a diameter of 1-1/2 degrees. NGC 6603 has a magnitude of 11.4 and a diameter of 4.5 minutes of arc.

The mystery of the identity of M24 seems to have been resolved by Kenneth G. Jones, in an article he published in *Sky & Telescope* magazine (March 1967). The conclusion he arrived at is that M24 is indeed the Star Cloud and not the star cluster NGC 6603. For the purpose of this book, the observation of M24 refers to the Star Cloud and not to NGC 6603.

Because of the brightness and size of M24, the naked eye can see it as a detached portion of the Milky Way in the Sagittarius region. I have found that a pair of binoculars give a most pleasing view of this object. A telescope with an exceptionally wide field of view is needed to do this object justice, while in a telescope with a narrow field, this star cloud tends to lose its identity and is somewhat less impressive.

M40 NOTE

This object, the double star Winnecke 4, is included in this book for those amateurs who wish to *complete* their observations of the Messier objects.

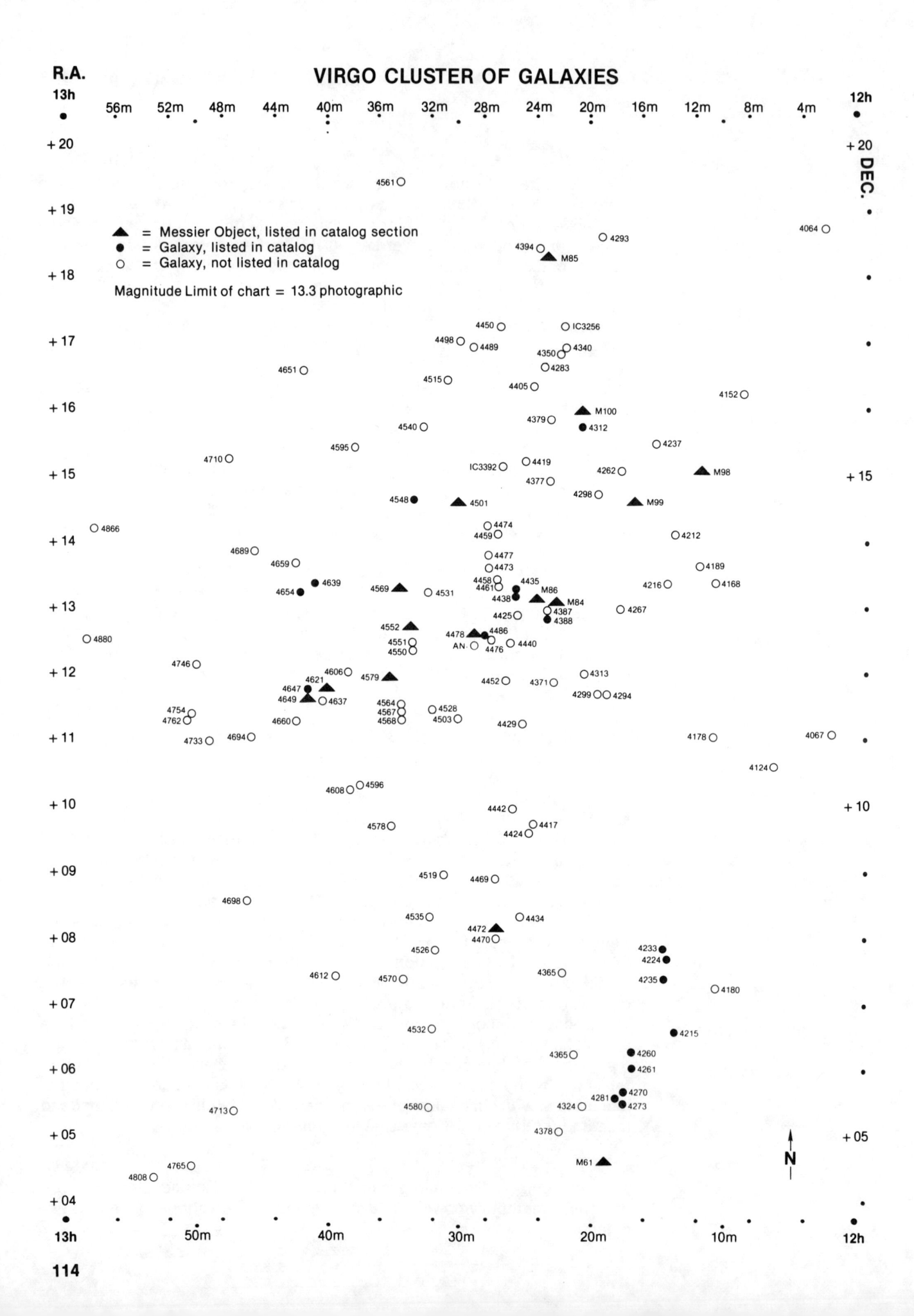

VIRGO CLUSTER OF GALAXIES

▲ = Messier Object, listed in catalog section
● = Galaxy, listed in catalog
○ = Galaxy, not listed in catalog

Magnitude Limit of chart = 13.3 photographic

VIRGO CLUSTER OF GALAXIES

NGC (IC**)	R.A.	DEC.	PHOTO MAG.	COMMENTS
4064	12h 01.7m	+ 18.43	12.5	
4067	12h 01.6m	+ 11.08	13.2	
4124	12h 05.6m	+ 10.39	12.7	4124 = IC3011
4152	12h 08.1m	+ 16.18	12.5	
4168	12h 09.8m	+ 13.29	12.7	
4178	12h 10.3m	+ 11.08	12.9	
4180	12h 10.5m	+ 07.19	13.2	
4189	12h 11.3m	+ 13.42	12.7	4189 = IC3050
*4192	12h 11.2m	+ 15.10	11.0	M98
4212	12h 13.1m	+ 14.11	11.9	
*4215	12h 13.3m	+ 06.40	13.0	
4216	12h 13.4m	+ 13.26	11.2	
*4224	12h 14.0m	+ 07.44	13.3	
*4233	12h 14.6m	+ 07.54	13.2	
*4235	12h 14.6m	+ 07.28	13.2	4235 = IC3098
4237	12h 14.7m	+ 15.36	12.3	
*4254	12h 16.3m	+ 14.42	10.2	M99
*4260	12h 16.8m	+ 06.22	13.1	
*4261	12h 16.8m	+ 06.06	12.0	
4262	12h 17.0m	+ 15.09	12.3	
4267	12h 17.2m	+ 13.05	12.4	
*4270	12h 17.3m	+ 05.45	13.3	
*4273	12h 17.5m	+ 05.37	12.3	
*4281	12h 17.8m	+ 05.40	12.5	
4293	12h 18.7m	+ 18.40	11.6	
4294	12h 18.8m	+ 11.47	12.6	
4298	12h 19.0m	+ 14.53	12.2	
4299	12h 19.1m	+ 11.47	12.8	
*4303	12h 19.3m	+ 04.45	10.9	M61
*4312	12h 20.0m	+ 15.49	12.9	
4313	12h 20.1m	+ 12.05	13.2	
*4321	12h 20.4m	+ 16.06	10.9	M100
4324	12h 20.5m	+ 05.32	12.5	
4339	12h 21.0m	+ 06.21	13.1	
4340	12h 21.1m	+ 17.00	12.4	
3256**	12h 21.1m	+ 07.20	13.0	
4350	12h 21.4m	+ 16.58	11.5	
4365	12h 21.9m	+ 07.35	11.5	
4371	12h 22.4m	+ 11.59	12.1	
*4374	12h 22.5m	+ 13.10	10.8	M84
4377	12h 22.7m	+ 15.02	12.5	
4378	12h 22.7m	+ 05.12	13.2	
4379	12h 22.7m	+ 15.54	12.6	
*4382	12h 22.9m	+ 18.28	10.2	M85
4283	12h 22.9m	+ 16.45	12.3	
4387	12h 23.2m	+ 13.05	13.2	
*4388	12h 23.3m	+ 12.56	12.2	
4394	12h 23.4m	+ 18.30	11.9	
4405	12h 23.6m	+ 16.28	12.9	4405 = IC0788
*4406	12h 23.7m	+ 13.14	10.9	M86
4417	12h 24.2m	+ 09.51	12.2	
4419	12h 24.4m	+ 15.19	11.6	

M24

NGC (IC**)	R.A.	DEC.	PHOTO MAG.	COMMENTS
4424	12h 24.7m	+ 09.42	13.1	
4425	12h 24.7m	+ 13.01	13.3	
4429	12h 24.9m	+ 11.23	11.4	
4434	12h 25.0m	+ 08.26	13.2	
*4435	12h 25.2m	+ 13.21	11.9	
*4438	12h 25.2m	+ 13.17	12.0	
4440	12h 25.4m	+ 12.34	13.0	
4442	12h 25.5m	+ 10.05	11.2	
4450	12h 25.9m	+ 17.21	11.2	
3392**	12h 26.2m	+ 15.16	13.3	
4452	12h 26.2m	+ 12.02	13.1	
4458	12h 26.4m	+ 13.31	13.3	
4459	12h 26.5m	+ 14.15	11.6	
4461	12h 26.5m	+ 13.28	12.2	
4469	12h 26.9m	+ 09.01	12.6	
4470	12h 27.0m	+ 08.06	12.9	
*4472	12h 27.2m	+ 08.16	10.2	M49
4473	12h 27.3m	+ 13.42	11.2	
4474	12h 27.4m	+ 14.21	12.6	
4476	12h 27.5m	+ 12.37	13.3	
4477	12h 27.5m	+ 13.55	11.9	
*4478	12h 27.8m	+ 12.36	12.2	
*4486	12h 28.3m	+ 12.40	10.4	M87
ZWG 070.141	12h 28.4m	+ 12.33	11.2	Very Compact
4489	12h 28.3m	+ 17.02	13.2	
4498	12h 29.1m	+ 17.08	12.8	

NGC (IC**)	R.A.	DEC.	PHOTO MAG.	COMMENTS
*4501	12h 29.4m	+14.42	10.6	M88
4503	12h 29.6m	+11.27	12.4	
4515	12h 30.5m	+16.32	13.3	
4519	12h 31.0m	+08.55	12.8	
4526	12h 31.5m	+07.58	10.6	
4528	12h 31.6m	+11.36	12.9	
4531	12h 31.8m	+13.21	13.3	
4532	12h 31.8m	+06.45	12.3	
4535	12h 31.8m	+08.28	11.1	
4540	12h 32.3m	+15.50	12.5	
*4548	12h 32.9m	+14.46	11.5	
4550	12h 33.0m	+12.30	12.5	
4551	12h 33.1m	+12.32	13.1	
*4552	12h 33.1m	+12.50	11.1	M89
4561	12h 33.6m	+19.36	12.7	
4564	12h 33.9m	+11.43	12.2	
4567	12h 34.0m	+11.32	12.5	
4568	12h 34.0m	+11.31	12.5	
*4569	12h 34.3m	+13.26	11.8	M90
4570	12h 34.3m	+07.31	11.8	
4578	12h 35.0m	+09.50	12.9	
*4579	12h 35.2m	+12.05	11.5	M58
4580	12h 32.2m	+05.38	13.1	
4595	12h 37.3m	+15.34	12.8	
4596	12h 37.4m	+10.27	12.4	
4606	12h 38.5m	+12.11	12.7	
4608	12h 38.7m	+10.25	12.6	
4612	12h 39.0m	+07.35	12.9	
*4621	12h 39.5m	+11.55	11.0	M59
4637	12h 40.3m	+11.43	12.2	4637 = 4638
*4639	12h 40.4m	+13.32	12.4	
*4647	12h 41.0m	+11.52	12.5	
*4649	12h 41.1m	+11.50	10.3	M60
4651	12h 41.3m	+16.40	11.3	
*4654	12h 41.4m	+13.25	11.8	
4659	12h 42.0m	+13.47	13.3	
4660	12h 42.0m	+11.28	12.1	
4689	12h 45.3m	+14.02	12.8	
4694	12h 45.8m	+11.15	12.4	
4698	12h 45.9m	+08.45	12.1	
4710	12h 47.2m	+15.26	11.6	
4713	12h 47.4m	+05.35	12.3	
4733	12h 48.6m	+11.11	13.2	
4746	12h 49.4m	+12.21	13.3	
4754	12h 49.8m	+11.35	11.6	
4762	12h 50.4m	+11.30	11.1	
4765	12h 50.7m	+04.44	13.0	
4808	12h 53.3m	+04.34	12.5	
4866	12h 57.0m	+14.27	11.9	
4880	12h 57.7m	+12.45	13.3	

* = Galaxies listed in the Catalog section.

ZWG = Zwicky Catalog of Galaxies & Clusters of Galaxies

FORNAX GALAXY GROUP

All NGC galaxies listed;

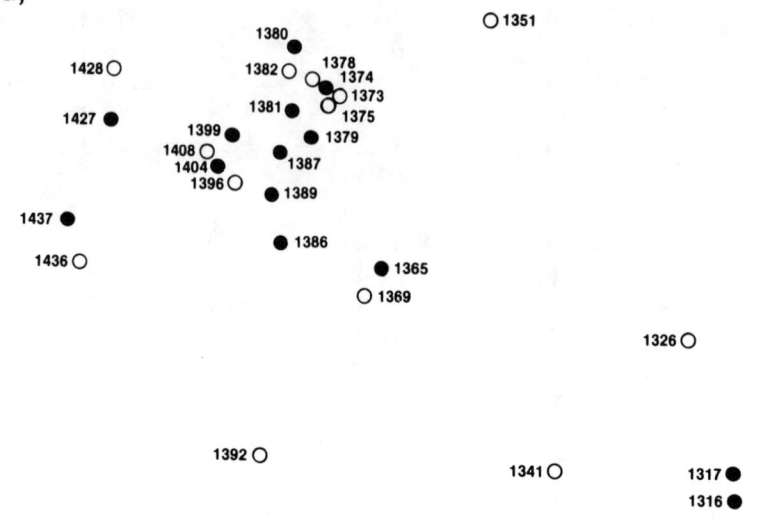

1351, 1380, 1428, 1382, 1378, 1374, 1373, 1427, 1381, 1375, 1399, 1379, 1408, 1387, 1404, 1396, 1389, 1437, 1386, 1436, 1365, 1369, 1326, 1392, 1341, 1317, 1316

Non-existant galaxies omitted;

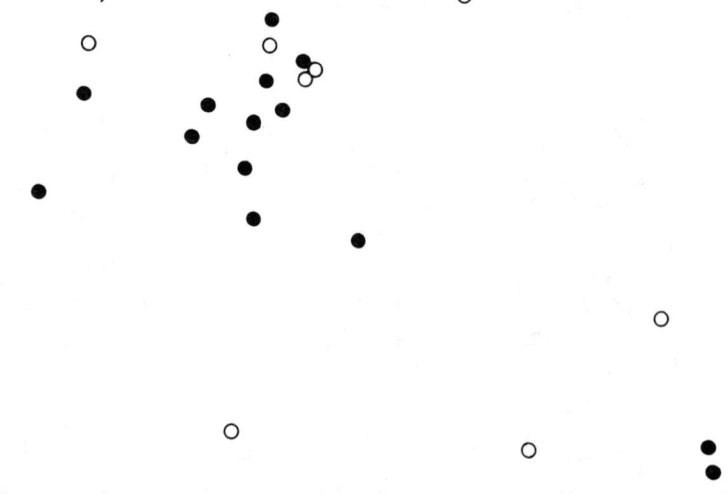

Galaxies listed in the catalog;

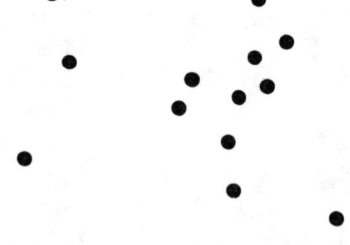

○ = Not included in book
● = Observation in book

FORNAX GALAXY GROUP

NAME	R.A.	DEC.	EXIST	PHOTO MAG.
NGC 1316	3h 20.78m	−37° 23.1	Yes	10.1
1317	3h 20.85m	−37° 16.9	Yes	12.2
1326	3h 22.5m	−36° 38.9	Yes	11.8
1341	3h 26.4m	−37° 19.3	Yes	13.1
1351	3h 28.6m	−35° 2	Yes	12.1
1365	3h 31.7m	−36° 18.3	Yes	11.2
1369	3h 32.6m	−36° 26.3	No*	—
1373	3h 33.18m	−35° 24.3	Yes	?
1374	3h 33.21m	−35° 23.8	Yes	12.4
1375	3h 33.21m	−35° 26.3	Yes	?
1378	3h 33.58m	−35° 22.4	No*	—
1379	3h 34.2m	−35° 24	Yes	12.3
1380	3h 34.52m	−35° 8.4	Yes	11.4
1381	3h 34.7m	−35° 28	Yes	12.6
1382	3h 34.36m	−35° 19.8	Yes	?
1386	3h 35m	−36° 10	Yes	12.4
1387	3h 35.1m	−35° 41	Yes	12.1
1389	3h 35.3m	−35° 55	Yes	12.8
1392	3h 36.48m	−37° 17.7	Yes	?
1396	3h 36.6m	−35° 50.1	No*	—
1399	3h 36.58m	−35° 36.7	Yes	10.9
1404	3h 37.0m	−35° 45	Yes	11.5
1408	3h 37.26m	−35° 41.2	No*	—
1427	3h 40.4m	−35° 34	Yes	12.4
1428	3h 40.5m	−35° 19	Yes	?
1436	3h 41.31m	−36° 16.9	No*	—
1437	3h 41.7m	−36° 1	Yes	12.9

* NGC catalog numbers have been assigned based on a report by the original observer. The number could not be confirmed at a later observation. We don't know what was observed—perhaps a comet or a mistaken position.

KEYS

TABLES

B	=	Barnard
B.N.	=	Bright Nebula
Bt.Kt.	=	Bright Knot
Bt.Nb.	=	Bright Nebula
Cl.	=	Cluster
DEC	=	Declination
D.N.	=	Dark Nebula
D.S.	=	Deep-Sky
Gal.	=	Galaxy
Gb.	=	Globular
h	=	Hour(s)
IC	=	Index Catalog
inv.	=	Involved
m	=	Minutes of Arc
n	=	Nebula
Nb.	=	Nebula
NGC	=	New General Catalog
Op.Cl.	=	Open Cluster
p	=	Photographic
Pl.Nb.	=	Planetary Nebula
R.A.	=	Rate of Acension
s	=	Seconds of Arc
S.P.	=	Skalnate Pleso Atlas of the heavens
st	=	Star(s)
v	=	Visual
var.	=	Variable

CATALOG SECTION

B.N.	=	Bright Nebula
Bt.Kt.	=	Bright Knot
Bt.Nb.	=	Bright Nebula
Cass.	=	Cassegrain
Cl.	=	Cluster
D.N.	=	Dark Nebular
E	=	Erfle
F/	=	Focal Length
G	=	Galoc ocular
Gal.	=	Galaxy
Gb.Cl.	=	Globular Cluster
Hy	=	Huyghenian ocular
in.	=	Inch(es)
K	=	Kellner ocular
Ko	=	Konig ocular
mm	=	Millimeter
mag.	=	Magnitude
n	=	Nebula
Nb.	=	Nebula
NGC	=	New General Catalog
neb	=	Nebula
O	=	Orthoscopic ocular
Op.Cl.	=	Open cluster
P	=	Plossl ocular
p	=	Photographic
Pl.	=	Planetary Nebula
Pl.Nb.	=	Planetary Nebula
RFL	=	Reflector telescope
RR	=	Refractor telescope
v	=	Visual
w/	=	With

GLOSSARY

ANNULAR	A ring shaped object.
ANOMAL	Abnormal, irregular.
AVERTED VISION	To look off to the side and not directly at the object.
BRIGHT NEBULA	An irregular, shapeless, often very large nebula. Also known as Bright Diffuse Nebulae.
CLUSTER	A group of stars, the members of which are closer to each other than the stars around them. Also known as Open Star Clusters.
DARK NEBULA	An irregular, shapeless, dark nebula. Usually referred to as a Barnard Object, e.g. B33.
DECLINATION	The angular distance of a celestial body from the celestial equator along the hour circle to the body. Measured in degrees, minutes and seconds through 90 degrees, and named north or south as the body is north or south of the celestial equator.
DEEP-SKY OBJECT	Refers to such object as: Bright Diffuse Nebulae, Dark Nebulae, Galaxies, Globular Clusters, Open Star Clusters and Planetary Nebulae.
DEGREE	1/360th part of a circle. It is used for measuring arcs or angles.
EYEPIECE	In a telescope, the lens system through which the observer views the image formed, and which magnifies that image for better and more efficient viewing. Modern eyepieces consist of a system of at least two lenses: the larger is called the field lens, while the smaller is the eye lens.
FIELD	The area visible through the lens system of the telescope. Also known as the field of view.
GALAXY	A large gravitational system of stars.
GLOBULAR CLUSTERS	A more compact group of stars, than the Open Star Cluster. They contain more stars and are usually a slightly flattened spherical shape.
HOMOGENEOUS	Of uniform structure or composition throughout.
INDEX CATALOG	A list of Deep-Sky Objects found after the New General Catalog was completed. Known as the IC
MINUTES	1/60th of an hour or a degree.
MOTTLING	An object having an uneven brightness; or having spots or blotches of different shades of brightness e.g. A galaxy showing brighter or darker (or both) areas.
NEW GENERAL CATALOG	A large list of Deep-Sky Objects, found visually by such early observers as the Herschels. Also known as the NGC.
OCULARS	See eyepiece.
PLANETARY NEBULA	A round or oval mass of nebulosity, usually having a central star which is very hot, and therefore much brighter photographically than visually.
RIGHT ASCENSION	A celestial coordinate; it is the angular distance measured from the vernal equinox eastward along the celestial equator to the

	hour circle of a given star or other celestial body. It is measured in degrees, from 0 to 360, or more commonly in hours, from 0 to 24.
SECONDS	1/60th of a minute.
SWEEPING	The art of moving the telescope's field back and forth, in an east—west direction. The next sweep will be a little north or south of the last one; while retaining some of the field from the last sweep. This way the telescope fields will overlap each other.
STAR ATLAS	A map showing the relative apparent positions of stars, deep-sky objects, etc., in the sky.
STAR CATALOG	A list of stars and deep-sky objects that indicate various characteristics and important data for each.

DEEP-SKY OBSERVERS CHECK LIST (BASIC)

Telescope with finderscope
Oculars and accessories (prism, diffraction grating, etc.)
*Star Charts along with photo copies of select objects or areas.
Binoculars
List of Objects to See (made prior to the observing)
Paper for recording observations, including field drawings.
Pencil for use above
Table used for holding above items (except telescope)
Flashlight with red lens
Optional:
   Clock
   Food & Drink
   Radio
   Tape Recorder

*Photo copies of photographs seen in an astronomical journal may help when trying to identify hard to find objects, such as a faint planetary (or a small stellarlike one), a faint galaxy, a small faint globular cluster in the galaxy M31...etc.

   Amateurs who may have questions, suggestions or comments of any kind *referring* to this book, or those who need assistance in observing, send a self addressed stamped envelope to:

Ronald J. Morales
c/o AZTEX Corporation
P O Box 50046
Tucson, AZ 85703-1046

RECOMMENDED READING

SUGGESTED BOOKS

Burnhams Celestial Handbooks, Vol. 1-3, Dover Pub., By Robert Burnham Jr.
Celestial Objects for Common Telescopes, Vol. 1, 2, Dover Pub., Reprint, By R.T. Webb
Deep-Sky Splendors, Sky Publishing Corp., By Hans Vehrenberg
Finest Deep-Sky Objects, Sky Publishing Corp., By Mullaney & McCall
Messier Album, Sky Publishing Corp., By Mallas & Kreimer
Messier's Nebulae & Star Clusters, American-Elsevier, Out Of Print, By Kenneth G. Jones.
Reference Catalog of Bright Galaxies, Univ. Texas Press, By DeVancouleurs & DeVancouleurs
Revised New General Catalog of Non-Stellar Objects, Univ. Arizona Press, By Tift & Sulentic
Telescope Handbook & Star Atlas, Thomas Y. Crowell Co., By N.E. Howard
Webb Society Handbooks, Vol. 1-5, Enslow Pub.

STAR ATLASES

AAVSO Variable Star Atlas, Sky Publishing Co., By Scovil
Atlas Stellarium (Photographic), Sky Publishing Co., By Hans Vehrenberg
Skalnate Pleso Atlas of the Heavens (& companion Star Catalog), By Antonin Becvar
Sky Atlas 2000.0 (& companion Catalogues), Sky Publishing Co., By W. Tirion
True Visual Magnitude Photographic Star Atlas, By Chris Popadopoulos

MAGAZINES

Astrograph Magazine, Astrograph Pub.
Astronomy Magazine, Astromedia Corp.
Deep-Sky Magazine, Astromedia Corp.
Sky & Telescope Magazine, Sky Publishing Corp.
Webb Society Journal, Webb Society

MAGAZINE ARTICLES

A Cross-Reference of Herschel Objects to the New General Catalog, **Deep-Sky Monthly**, Sept. 1970, By Walter Scott Houston
Adventures in Deep-Sky Astronomy Observing with Binoculars, **Deep-Sky Monthly**, July 1980, By Kevin Ritschel
Adventures in the Virgo Cloud, **Sky & Telescope**, Feb. 1955, By Leland S. Copeland
A Messier Album (Seperate Installments), **Sky & Telescope**, May 1967 to Sept. 1970, By John Mallas & E. Kreimer
An Introduction to Small Telescopes, **Astronomy**, July 1974, By Alan E. Nourse
An Observers Guide to the Orion Nebula, **Sky & Telescope**, Jan. 1963, By John Mallas
50 Celestial Splendors to View, **Sky & Telescope**, Jan. 1981, By Walter S. Houston
Finest Deep-Sky Objects (Seperate Installments), **Sky & Telescope**, Nov. 1965, By Wallace & McCall
Get Ready for the Virgo Cluster, **Astronomy**, March 1983, By David J. Eicher
Learning to Look, **Astronomy**, Sept. 1979, By Robert Burnham
Lord Rosse's Observations Compared With Those Made Using Modern Large Reflectors, **Webb Society Quarterly Journal No. 48**, April 1982, By Malcolm J. Thomson
Masking Apertures for Deep-Sky Study, **Deep-Sky Monthly**, March 1980, By Vern Burns
Observing Diffuse Nebulae, **Astronomy**, July 1980, By F. Michael Witkoski
Observing Details in Galaxies, **Deep-Sky Monthly**, April 1981, By David J. Eicher
Observing for Pleasure, **Astronomy**, Nov. 1981, By Michael Covington
Observing Galaxies, **Astronomy**, May 1976, By Richard Berry
Observing Galaxies Visually—I, **Sky & Telescope**, Nov. 1979, By Ronald J. Buta
Observing Galaxies Visually—II, **Sky & Telescope**, Dec. 1979, By Ronald J. Buta
Observing Nebulae & Clusters, **Astronomy**, Jan. 1974, By Thomas C. Bretl
Observing Planetary Nebulae, **Astronomy**, Aug. 1977, By Tom Reiland
Observing Planetary Nebulae, **Astronomy**, June 1981, By F. Michael Witkoski
Observing with Binoculars, **Astronomy**, June 1977, By Henry J. Phillips
Richfield Telescopes, **Astronomy**, June 1975, By Thomas C. Bretl
Searching for Supernovae, **Astronomy**, April 1982, By F. Michael Witkoski

RECOMMENDED READING

MAGAZINE ARTICLES

Spiral Structure in Galaxies—the historical perspective, **Webb Society Quarterly Journal No. 42**, Oct. 1980, By Steven J. Hynes
The Pleasures of Deep-Sky Observing, **Astronomy**, Sept. 1981, By David J. Eicher
Tune Up Your Telescope, **Astronomy**, Dec. 1975, By Thomas C. Bretl
What You Can See Through a Small Refractor, **Astronomy**, June 1976, By Henry J. Phillips
Your Most Valuable Equipment, **Astronomy**, April 76, By Richard Berry

TELESCOPES & ACCESSORIES

AD Libs Astronomics
2401 Tee Circle—Suite 105
Norman, Oklahoma 73069

Astronomy New England, Inc.
215 Highland Street
Holliston, Massachusetts 01746

Bushnell
2828 E. Foothill Boulevard
Pasadena, California 91107

Celestron International
2835 Columbia Street
P O Box 3578-A
Torrance, California 90503

Chicago Optical & Supply Co.
Box 11309
Chicago, Illionis 60611

Cosmic Connections Inc.
1460 N. Farnsworth Avenue
Aurora, Illionis 60505

Coulter Optical Co.
P O Box K
Idyllwild, California 92349

Crown Optics Inc.
P O Box 8672
Newport Beach, California 92660

Dixie Telescopes
290 Hilderbrand Drive-Suite B-8
Atlanta, Georgia 30328

Edmund Scientific Co.
101 E. Gloucester Pike T229
Barrington, New Jersey 08007

Edwin Hirsch
168 Lakeview Drive
Tomkins Cove, New York 10986

The Image Point
831 N. Swan
Tucson, Arizona 85713

A. Jaegers
691 S Merrick Road
Lynbrook, New York 11563

LUMICON
2111 Research Drive #5
Livemore, California 94550

Meade Instruments Corp.
1675 Toronto Way
Costa Mesa, California 92626

Meade Trading Co., Inc.
13585 N.E. Whitaker Way
Portland, Oregon 97230

B.E. Meyers & Co.
17525 N.E. 67th Court
Redmond, Washington 98052

North Star Telescope Co.
3542 Elm Street
Toledo, Ohio 43608

Kenneth F. Novak & Co.
Box 69v
Ladysmith, Wisconsin 54848

Optron Systems
704 Charcot Avenue
San Jose, California 95131

Orion Telescopes
P O Box 1158-T
Santa Cruz, California 95061

Parks Company
679 Easy Street—Suite B
Simi Valley, California 93065

Questar
Box C—Dept 105
New Hope, Pennsylvania 18938

R.V.R. Optical
P O' Box 62
East Chester, New York 10709

Scott Optical
4628 E. Cornell
Fresno, California 93703

Star Instruments
3641 E. Fox Lair Drive
Flagstaff, Arizona 86001

Star Quest Enterprise
378 S. Tustin Avenue
Orange, California 92666

Star Tracker
3093 Walnut
Boulder, Colorado 80302

Starliner Co.
1106 S. Columbus
Tucson, Arizona 85711

Telescopics
P O Box 98
LaCanada, California 91011

Televue
15A Green Hill Lane
Spring Valley, New York 10977

Texas Nautical Repair Co.
3209 Milam
Houston, Texas 77006

Tomlin Industries Inc.
679 Easy Street
Simi Valley, California 93065

Roger W. Tuthill Inc.
11 Tanglewood Lane
Box 1086 Street
Mountainside, New Jersey 07092

University Optics
2122 E Delhi Road
P O Box 1205
Ann Arbor, Michigan 48106

Wack Electronics
5722 W North Avenue
Milwaukee, Wisconsin 53208

DEEP-SKY OBJECTS FOUND

NAME	DATE	TELESCOPE	OCULAR	SEEING	COMMENTS

DEEP-SKY OBJECTS FOUND

NAME	DATE	TELESCOPE	OCULAR	SEEING	COMMENTS

FAILED TO SEE LIST

NAME	DATE	TELESCOPE	OCULAR	SEEING	COMMENTS

Note: Objects on the *Failed to See List* should be searched for again with the same telescope when the seeing is better or with a larger aperture telescope.

FAILED TO SEE LIST

NAME	DATE	TELESCOPE	OCULAR	SEEING	COMMENTS

Note: Objects on the *Failed to See List* should be searched for again with the same telescope when the seeing is better or with a larger aperture telescope.